ENCOUNTERS WITH
THE EVER-PRESENT GOD

ENCOUNTERS WITH THE EVER-PRESENT GOD

HOWARD W. ROBERTS

THE
PILGRIM
PRESS

Cleveland

The Pilgrim Press, 700 Prospect Avenue East, Cleveland, Ohio 44115-1100

pilgrimpress.com

Printed in the United States of America on acid-free paper

06 05 04 03 02 01   5 4 3 2 1

Library of Congress Cataloging-in-Publication Data

Roberts, Howard W., 1947–
        Encounter with the ever-present God / Howard W. Roberts.
              p.   cm.
        Includes bibliographical references.
        ISBN 0-8298-1435-3 (alk. paper)
        1. Incarnation.   I. Title.
BT220 .R62   2001
231.—dc21

                                                            2001053184

CONTENTS

PREFACE

My uncle would have said that the word *incarnation* is a fifty-cent word. It is one of those words that gets tossed around in seminary classes and sometimes tossed out in sermons. Hearers may or may not connect with the word. An image may or may not come to their minds that helps them translate the concept with meaning for them.

The best way I know to define incarnation is with a story. A young boy was awakened in the middle of the night by the clap of thunder in the midst of a storm. He was frightened and burst into tears. His mother heard his cries and went to his room to comfort him. After several minutes of holding him and rubbing his back, the mother sensed her son was calming down and had ceased crying. She began to make overtures to leave him and return to her bed. His anxiety began to rise again and his mother sought to reassure him. She said, "Bret, there is nothing to be afraid of. Besides, God will be with you." Bret replied, "I know God will be with me, but I need somebody with a skin face."

The incarnation means to put a skin face on God. Incarnation means the enfleshment, indwelling, of God in human beings. Marcus Borg's approach in *The God We Never Knew* is helpful to me. His understanding of panentheism expresses the concept of God's presence and involvement in the human enterprise in a way that is helpful to me. Panentheism means that God is in everything. God is not to be equated with the sum of everything but is more than everything. God is in everything and we are within God.[1] This is different from pantheism, which identifies the universe with God. Panentheism understands God to be in everything but also more than everything so that God is not equated with the universe and all that is in it.

I have been grappling with what it means for God to be involved in the human enterprise for more than half my life. I have wrestled with questions about why there are so many religions and what distinguishes one from another. I've wondered if there was anything unique about Christianity. For nearly forty years, I have sought to interpret and reinterpret the meaning of Christmas in Christianity. Learning about the Christian year and the season of Advent helped me in my struggle and focus.

One of the results of my grappling, interpreting, struggling, and learning has been to experience for myself and encourage others to examine how, when, where, and why the biblical stories intersect with our stories. I have found it valuable to stop, look, and listen at these intersections. The experience of encountering God at these intersections is part of the mystery and majesty of the incarnation. In the pages that follow, I explore what happens when people encounter God, using a variety of biblical situations and characters to illustrate reactions of people when they realize they are in the presence of God. I have discovered that my reactions and those of many of my contemporaries are similar to those in the biblical accounts.

The thread woven throughout this book is that God comes to the world through people. We usually react to God's presence like people before us have reacted and like those around us react. Jesus said of himself, "I am the light of the world." Later, he said to his disciples, "You are the light of the world." Which is it? It is both. God comes to us, seeking to get under our skin and into our skin because God comes to the world in a "skin face." This approach by God is painted throughout the biblical material, but the clearest portrait is the composite of Jesus portrayed by the gospel writers. My purpose in this book is to explore how God has come to people in the biblical accounts and then to build bridges from the biblical lives to contemporary lives. May you discover how, when, where, and why God comes to the world with love in you and through you as you travel with me on this journey through the following pages.

ENCOUNTERS WITH
THE EVER-PRESENT GOD

WHEN GOD ARRIVES
JOHN 1:1–18

Biblical faith affirms that God existed before the creation of the world and that God has been actively involved in what was created from the beginning. John (1:1) uses the term *Word* to identify the creative force of God and to assert the eternity, proximity, and identity of the Word with God. John 1:1–5 and Genesis 1:1–5 are very similar. In both passages, God's Word created a world in which light and darkness were differentiated. God's Word created a world in which the Word participates.

God has been involved in creation from the outset, bringing the gifts of hope, peace, love, and joy to the creation. Inherent in the nature of gifts is that they be received. As God has given gifts to the world, God has received a mixed response and reception. The progression of response when God arrives is that life continues as usual, fear arises, good news is announced, and thanksgiving is offered. Join me in exploring how these were typical responses to the birth of Jesus and how they are universal responses when, where, and how God arrives.

LIFE CONTINUES AS USUAL

We are not getting the whole story if people suggest that as soon as they encounter God, all of life changes instantly for the better. This is not true of any of the biblical characters, and it is not true of us today. We do not know how long Abraham, after encountering God, continued to live in Ur of the Chaldeans before he decided to go out, not knowing where he was going. Some years later there remained a residue of the desire of Abraham for life to continue as usual. The evidence is in Abraham's struggle with his understanding of God's invitation to offer Isaac as a sacrifice.

An even earlier example is Noah. How long did Noah go on as usual before he started gathering the lumber, hammer, and nails for the ark?

Abraham and Noah are just two of the many biblical stories recording God's arrival in the midst of people. Often the attitude of the people was for life to continue as usual, at least for a while. There is ample evidence that God's arrival makes no difference in people's lives.

The birth of Jesus has come to be the most important statement for Christians about God's arrival. Twenty centuries of tradition have enhanced our emphasis on the birth of Jesus. Tradition also has enabled us to wrap up all of the events in a neat religious package with no loose ends. Plenty of evidence supports the thesis that after the birth of Jesus, life continued as it had prior to his birth. Rome continued with its census taking. Tradesmen in Bethlehem continued to enjoy a booming business because of the additional travelers. The soldiers had all they could handle simply maintaining order. Joseph and Mary, especially Mary, had a restless night or two. A few shepherds thought they heard something unusual out on the Judean hillside, and it seemed as though one star shown more brightly than the others. But, basically, life continued as usual when God came to the world. Is it any different today when God arrives on the scene?

December 25th is the date that the majority of Christians celebrate the Word becoming flesh. The date is arbitrary. We do not know when Jesus was born. We use December 25th as the date to affirm, "the Word became flesh and dwelt among us" (Jn. 1:14 RSV). The elusiveness of dating the birth of Christ illustrates that God is always present and that God is continuing to arrive. Only the Eternal can be present and arriving simultaneously.

Identifying exactly when God arrives in a person's life really cannot be done. One can only bear witness that God has arrived. Events, circumstances, and thought processes often heighten one's consciousness of God. But identifying the time when God arrives is a matter of perspective and perception.

A television broadcaster told of taking his show on the road and would often dialogue with the audience after the show. On occasion, he would hold up a ball and ask what color it was. Someone would respond, "Black." Others would agree. The broadcaster would say, "Right. From your point of view the ball is black. Yet, from the point of view of those of us on the platform, the ball is white. If you insist that what you see is right and we insist that what we see is right, we can get nowhere. You might overcome us with power or bullets, but (turning the ball around) we now see the ball is both black and white." Our perception of when and how God arrives is just as difficult and depends greatly upon perspective.

We may be insensitive to or deny God's presence in the world and in our lives. Such feelings and conclusions do not mean that God does not come to us; rather, these feelings and conclusions mean that we are not responding positively as God comes to us. It is common for our lives to continue as usual in the presence of God. We often are oblivious that we are standing on holy ground.

We expect that the arrival of God would at least receive a response similar to what we expect when we arrive. Who of us, arriving at a place, does not at least anticipate that someone will acknowledge our arrival? What about when you arrive at work or get home from school? Do you not expect that someone will acknowledge your arrival with a smile, a hello, or at least a grunt? Of course, if we were orchestrating our own arrival scenes, we would have "Pomp and Circumstance" played, bugles blaring, and all eyes focused on us.

Consider what you are wearing today. Did you not choose your outfit because you thought it enhanced your appearance and would cause people to notice you when you arrived? Who of us does not brighten up when someone acknowledges our arrival?

We lull ourselves into continuing life as usual when God arrives by expressing our conviction that God is always present. While that is true, our lives do not advertise such a belief. Because we often do not know *how* God arrives, we conclude we cannot know *when* God arrives. Part of our expectation of how God comes is related to anticipation of fanfare and attention getting that would be our approach if we were in charge. We want the spectacular. If something extraordinary would happen, then we would know God had arrived. Jesus said, "I was hungry" (Mt. 25:35), and we respond with indignation, "When did we see you hungry and not feed you?" We claim that if God would just walk down the aisle, we would accept God and our faith would be increased. God comes down the aisle looking a lot like you or me or George Burns (like in the movie *Oh God!*), and our lives continue as usual.

Would you not expect that if God were in charge of the whole universe that God would have orchestrated a grand entrance for Jesus of Nazareth? Do we not equate the presence of greatness with some display of the spectacular? If nothing spectacular occurs, we conclude that, apparently, no one great is present. We could draw such a conclusion from the matter-of-fact Gospel accounts of the birth of Jesus. John wrote, "He was in the world, and the world was made through him, yet the world knew him not. He came to his own home, and his own people received him not" (Jn. 1:10–11 RSV). Luke says, "And she gave birth to her first-born son and wrapped him in swaddling cloths, and laid him in a manger, because there was no place for them in the inn" (Lk. 2:7 RSV). Matthew just gives the facts: "Now when Jesus was born in Bethlehem of Judea in the days of Herod the king, behold, wise men from the East came to Jerusalem" (Mt. 2:1 RSV). Mark gives no account of the birth of Jesus. Isn't it amazing that so little was made of such a great arrival? Is this evidence that when God arrives life continues as usual?

The Moffatt translation (the work of Scottish translator James Moffatt) of the first chapter of Luke has an unusual word applied to Jesus. Jesus is described as the dawn. Have you ever noticed how quietly and unobtrusively the dawn arrives? How many of us stop to acknowledge that dawn has come? Many of us miss the dawn because we sleep through it. When the dawn does arrive, we throw a shoe at the clock or cover our heads, trying to convince ourselves that the new day has not yet arrived. The dawn is the beginning of a new day, with its corollaries of beauty and power, revealing itself to the world around us. The old day has gone and has been lost in the night; a new beauty unfolds, and a new power makes itself felt.

Is this not descriptive of Jesus? He dawned upon the world. We begin to sense and feel freshness, newness, as dawn arrives. As the dawn, Christ came to give light and direction to those who sit in darkness. But any one of us can shut out the dawn. Just close your eyes and there is darkness. We, like the people of the first century, may respond to the arrival of God by continuing life as usual.

In a sermon, "Religion of the Dawn," preached at City Temple in London on Easter 1955, Leslie Weatherhead identified Christianity as the religion of the dawn, because it has a dawn answer for every situation. It does not pretend there is no night. Christianity is a religion of unquenchable faith and hope and patience. It is unquenchable because it believes that the permanent thing is light and the passing thing is darkness; that however long the night, whether it be in world affairs or in the poignant, private world of the human heart, the night will pass. All affairs, private and worldwide, are in the hands of God who is in complete and final control and who has decreed the entire conquest of evil and the final emergence of indescribable good. Christianity is like the dawn dispelling slavery, disease, destruction, hunger, poverty, war, homelessness, ignorance, and injustice.

God's arrival is a surprise, not because God is attempting to trick or confuse us, but because we usually have preconceived ideas of how God will arrive and to whom God will appear. Who would ever have dreamed that God would come as a baby? Who would expect anything out of a baby except crying and demands? Generally, only parents, grandparents, and a few of their very close friends see any significance at all in the birth of a child. Babies do not make an impact on the things that seem to really make a difference in the world, such as space flights, stock markets, political campaigns, wars, and a few inventions.

About two centuries ago, people were following the march of Napoleon and waiting for news of the wars. And all the while, in their homes, babies were being born. But who could think about babies? Everybody was thinking about battles.

In one year, midway between Trafalgar and Waterloo, there stole into the world a host of heroes. William Gladstone was born in Liverpool; Alfred, Lord Tennyson, at the Somerset rectory; and Oliver Wendell Holmes in Massachusetts; and the same day of that same year, Charles Darwin made his debut at Shrewsbury, and Abraham Lincoln drew his first breath in Kentucky. Music was enriched by the advent of Felix Mendelssohn in Hamburg.

But nobody thought of babies; everybody was thinking of battles. Yet, which of the battles of 1809 mattered more than the babies of 1809? We fancy that God can only manage the world with big battalions, when all the while beautiful babies are doing it. When a wrong needs righting, a truth needs preaching, a continent needs opening, justice needs doing, or mercy needs sharing, God appears as a baby to do it.

How does God come to people? God comes to people through people. God redeems humanity through humanity. How is God coming to you right now? You will encounter God in the face of a child, the voices of a choir, the hollow eyes of a lonely woman, the frail frame of a hungry man, the cheerful word of a close friend, the warmth of a caring family.

As God arrives today, the Creator comes as the Redeemer comes, every day, quietly, unobtrusively; yet, many of us will sleep through God's coming. When God came in Jesus' birth so long ago, there was no immediate difference. Life continued as usual. A few shepherds went to a stable, but that was nothing spectacular. Later some wise men traveled to gaze at the child, but it's natural for adults to gaze at small children. An insecure Herod felt threatened by an infant. All of this passed. Soon life was back to normal. Eventually, Joseph, Mary, and Jesus settled into the routine of life in Nazareth. Most people finally forgot that Jesus was the child who came too early. Much later, as events in Jesus' life transpired resulting in his death and resurrection, interest developed in remembering and retelling about his birth.

What difference will God's coming make to you as God arrives in your life today? I suspect your first response will be to continue life as usual.

FEAR ARISES

As your consciousness of God's arrival heightens, fear arises. Fear is a universal reaction to the awareness of God's presence. Fear is an internal response to a real or imagined danger that threatens the emotional, spiritual, or physical well-being of a person. Fear is one of the earliest feelings we experience. Infants have a fear of falling, a fear of being abandoned, and a fear of loud noises. What parents have not been disturbed when leaving their child of eight or nine months of age in someone else's hands? Previously, the child has been left before without incident, but this time the child obviously is upset at being left. What is happening? The child's consciousness is developing. Now the child associates the presence of a strange face, the childcare provider, with the soon-to-be-absent parents. Later, at about eighteen months of age, the child will show some fear of being left well in advance of the event occurring. The child probably will cling more at that time, anticipating being left and fearing what may happen. Fear gets an early start in our lives. Even when God arrives in our lives, the presence of God is greeted by our fear.

Fear surfaces quickly in our lives because security and self-preservation are important to us. We associate our security with what is routine and expected. Anything that alters the order of life as we have come to experience it is threatening, frightening, and fear-producing. Luke wrote that this is what happened to Mary, the mother of Jesus.

Mary was young, but her life was developing along an anticipated course. She had been betrothed to Joseph. Betrothal lasted for one year and was as binding as marriage. Betrothal could be dissolved only by divorce. There is evidence that Joseph was much older than Mary was, but perhaps that provided a greater sense of stability and security for her. Mary and Joseph were making wedding plans. Although it also represented a change, marriage offered stability and security. Marriage was the expected direction in which a young woman was to move. Insecurity and fear arose if a girl in ancient Palestine became too old (late teens) and was not betrothed. Mary's life was in order.

Gabriel paid a visit to Nazareth, and specifically to Mary. Gabriel is identified as a messenger from God and perhaps is the most famous angel. Often the word *messenger* is translated from the Hebrew and Greek into English as "angel." That is unfortunate for many people because then the imagery of wings and halo get in their way of comprehending the message the messenger brings. There is no way to know what Gabriel looked like, but it was not his appearance that disturbed Mary. It was the message he brought that was frightening. Luke said that Mary was deeply troubled by the messenger's message (Lk. 1:29).

The name Gabriel means "man of God." There is a Gabriel mentioned in Daniel (8:16), where he appears in a vision as a man. He functions as a revealer in that passage. The New Testament references show Gabriel as both a revealer and one who brings reassurance. Perhaps he brought reassurance out of necessity. Maybe the message he delivered so disarmed people that they felt vulnerable and unprotected. Gabriel must have sensed Mary's fear because he said, "Rejoice! The Lord is with you and has greatly favored you" (Lk. 1:28, author's translation [AT]). Without Mary saying a word, Gabriel hastened to add, "Do not be afraid" (Lk. 1:30 RSV). Maybe Gabriel was trembling with fear himself to think that the whole future of creation hung now on the answer of a girl. To Gabriel, Mary seemed hardly old enough to have a child, let alone *this* child. Perhaps Gabriel was talking to himself as much as he was to Mary when he said, "Don't be afraid."

But what was so frightening to Mary about Gabriel's message? After all, the message contained the promise that God would be with her. This promise was frightening because it unlocked the future to unknown and unlimited possibilities. Freedom is more frightening than slavery. When people are enslaved, they know exactly what is expected of them and what they are to do. They do not have to think for themselves, and they are not responsible for any decisions other than to obey their master. Many slaves remained on the plantations following the Civil War and continued to function as slaves because they were too frightened to leave and be on their own. Freedom is frightening because the possibilities are unlimited and unknown.

Mary's religious heritage was replete with people who had been frightened and disturbed by the presence of God. When God arrives, fear arises. God promised to be with Abraham, and the result was that Abraham pulled up stakes, left family, went to an unknown land, and tried to get established. It was with fear and trembling in the presence of God that Abraham had made such a decision. Later on, it was Moses who was frightened by God's arrival. Moses had gotten a steady job in Midian, married, settled down, and had two sons. Life was in order for him. One day while on the backside of the wilderness, he saw a strange-looking bush. His curiosity got the best of him, and he went over to examine it. The result was that Moses covered his face because he was afraid to look at God (Exod. 3:6). Before very long, Moses was leaving his family, traipsing off to Egypt, pleading, debating, arguing, and demanding that Pharaoh release his relatives from slavery and bondage. All of this got started back on the hillside with God's arrival and Moses' response of fear. Much later in Israel's history, Isaiah was at worship in the Temple. He reported what he heard and saw: "I saw the Lord" (Isa. 6:1). To Isaiah, it felt like the foundations of the Temple were shaking. Maybe it was the foundations of his life that were shaking. In any case, Isaiah was frightened when he sensed that God had arrived. He verbalized his fear: "There is no hope for me! I am doomed because every word that passes my lips is sinful and I live among a people whose every word is sinful" (Isa. 6:5 AT). The next thing Isaiah knew, he was experiencing the cleansing of God and beginning to confront his people with their need to encounter the living God and change the direction in which their lives were moving.

Is it any wonder, with this kind of history of encounters with the living God, that Mary was frightened when God arrived in her life? About the only thing Mary could expect from God was the unexpected. That in itself is frightening. Fearful feelings usually are heightened when there is a general threat to a person's existence by an unknown factor. People's anxiety levels often are much higher as they prepare to undergo medical tests than after they know the results, even when the results indicate a terminal disease. People cope better when a specific issue is identified and can be named. There is a sense that Mary had more reason to be frightened after she received the total message than prior to receiving it. She was pregnant, unmarried, and certain of what most people in Nazareth would say about her. However, as Luke reported the story, it seems that Mary's fear subsided some after she knew the facts. She said, "Behold, I am the handmaid of the Lord; let it be to me according to your word" (Lk. 1:38 RSV).

When God arrives, fear arises. The positive side of fear is awe. This is the primary concept that is identified as fear in the biblical material. Awe is a feeling response that has a mixture of reverence, respect, uneasiness, and wonder caused by something majestic or sublime. Awe is a response to being in the presence of power.

Fear arises in our lives when God arrives. Our knowledge that we have sinned is part of the cause of the fright. It is frightening for the unholy to be in the presence of the holy. This partially explains Moses' response at the burning bush and Isaiah's response in the Temple. Their feelings of awe resulted from their reverence and respect for God.

Fear arises when God arrives because no one knows what may happen. We have been inundated by so many unbiblical ideas about God that we attribute destructiveness to God more readily than we do creativeness. We believe much more quickly in original sin than we do in original goodness. We tend to conclude that any creativity God had was depleted when the world was created. Do you believe that God is still creating? Are you allowing God to be creative in your life and with your life?

This is where life gets frightening for many of us, when it really ought to get exciting. We never know where life will lead when God becomes involved in it. That is what is so frightening for many of us because we want each step and phase of life clearly marked. It is fairly easy to have religion, but it is very difficult to have faith. What is involved is deciding whether we are willing to bet our whole lives on God. We know that God's ways are not our ways, and that is frightening. The idea of faith is being certain that God's promise will be kept, but being uncertain as to how and when and by what means all of this will come to pass. Fear arises because we do not and cannot know all that this faith involves or requires. It is much easier to give verbal assent to this faith than it is to give living commitment to it.

Several years ago, I read about a man who decided he would walk a tightrope across Niagara Falls. He began to practice in his backyard. The next-door neighbor saw him and inquired as to what he was doing. The adventurer was reluctant to share his intention, not knowing how the neighbor would react, but he decided to let him in on his dream. To the adventurer's surprise, his neighbor was excited and enthusiastic and proceeded to encourage him toward his goal. Every time the adventurer would have second thoughts and start getting cold feet, his neighbor would say, "You can do it. I know you can. I have confidence in you. Keep practicing." Finally the day came. The rope was stretched across the Falls and the man crossed over successfully, to the excited cheers of onlookers. As so often happens, one conquest leads to the desire for another. It is intoxicating. The conqueror seeks a second, more spectacular feat than his first. This happened to this tightrope adventurer. He decided he would push a man in a wheelbarrow across the tightrope. Once again he began to prepare. His neighbor was right behind him, encouraging him every day. His expressions of confidence kept the venture going. One night the adventurer became discouraged and frightened. He decided to call off the whole thing. His neighbor protested, "You can do it. Don't stop now. You've done it once. I know you can do it again." To which the tightrope walker responded, "Do you really believe I can?" The neighbor replied, "Of course I do." To which the adventurer responded, "Okay, then I want you to be the one to ride in the wheelbarrow." At that moment fear arose in the neighbor because faith ceased to be an intellectual exercise and called for a living commitment.

Fear arose when God arrived in Mary's life, but she allowed her fear to give way to faith as she decided to faith her way into the future. Her statement, "I am the handmaid of the Lord," is an affirmation of her faithing. Her fear subsided but, apparently, did not completely dissipate because she hurried out of town for an extended visit with Elizabeth. Faith does not remove or replace all doubt and fear once and for all. Faith enables a person to see fear and doubt in proper perspective and faith provides the resources with which to cope with fear and doubt. Who knows what would have happened without Mary's ability to faith it? Just imagine the difficulty, the struggle, and the pain she encountered during the next thirty-three years. Certainly fear arose again and again, but her heritage and her experience taught her to faith it. That meant she could expect the unexpected from God and that the unexpected action and activity of God would be on the side of creativity, expansiveness, and freedom.

What about you and me? What happens to us when God arrives in our lives? One of the things that happens to us is that fear arises. We cannot imagine what is going to happen and that is unnerving. In such a circumstance, my son once said, "It nervouses me." That certainly identifies my feelings. However, if biblical religion is any indication of what may happen when God arrives, I suspect that my wildest dreams of what will happen when God arrives are not half-wild enough. Sarah spent her ninety-first birthday laughing. She never dreamed of giving birth to a child at her age. Nathaniel laughed at the idea that anything good could come out of Nazareth. If God could bring Isaac out of Sarah and Jesus out of Nazareth, then who are we who see through dark glasses to say what can and cannot be? There is a radical difference between the past and the future. The past is closed and the future is open. What has been is most emphatically not the full measure of what can be.

Nathaniel allowed the past to totally dominate his view of the future. He concluded that since nothing stupendous ever had happened in Nazareth, then nothing could or would. Does that sound like you? When was the last time you allowed your view of the past to dominate your view of the future so much that you concluded nothing good could ever come?

God comes to us and our fear level rises. We never know what God is going to do or what God is going to expect of us. God's presence is frightening, but once we learn to faith it, our fear subsides. Chances are our dreams have not been half wild enough. What we need to do when God arrives is to get in God's wheelbarrow. About the only thing we can safely expect from God is the unexpected, that God will do something bigger, better, and wilder than we ever dreamed. The surprises are unlimited once we get over the fear of God's arrival.

GOOD NEWS IS ANNOUNCED

Good news is announced when God arrives. But good news is disturbing. What a paradox! We anticipate, in our imaginations, that any good news would be met with pure delight and sheer joy, but it is not. Good news receives a mixed reaction. Often we conclude there is good news and bad news wrapped in the same message. We anticipate when, what, and how good news will come. We are thrown off balance when it does not come in the form or on the schedule we imagined. In baseball, the batter awaits the pitch. He anticipates a fastball in the strike zone. The pitcher releases the ball, the batter strides into the ball. He hesitates mentally as he determines that the pitch is a change-up rather than a fastball. It is in the strike zone and the batter takes a feeble swing at the ball. The batter was off balance because he allowed his anticipation to determine what he expected. He was momentarily blinded to any other possibilities and he missed the pitch.

Good news is announced when God arrives. The announcement is disturbing because it has ingredients we did not anticipate and we are thrown off balance. We are momentarily blinded to any good news other than what we consider and expect to be good news. God never arrives completely and solely as we expect—not because God is attempting to trick us, but because God's ways are not our ways. We want God's action to conform to our anticipation. Fortunately, God's action is not limited to our vision.

There are two constants evident in the good news that is announced by God's arrival. First, God is on the side of the oppressed seeking to liberate, to redeem, and to deliver those who are enslaved, regardless of what form the enslavement and oppression take. Second, people deliver the good news of God to people. The message and medium of the good news of God remain constant.

The good news of God seems to throw people off balance in spite of these two constant factors. The people were thrown off balance in Luke's record of the arrival of God in Jesus of Nazareth. Apparently, what was so unbalancing was what the news was and to whom it was delivered.

The message was that a *savior* was born. People in all ages, and in every age, look for a savior, but savior is a misnomer for what people are looking for. People want a rescuer rather than a redeemer. Too many interpret savior to mean a firefighter who rushes in at great risk to snatch the individual from the flames just before being engulfed by the heat and smoke. A better understanding of the biblical concept of savior is *redeemer*. In the ancient world, savior was primarily a deliverer from disease, danger, or human predicament in the world. Rulers, both Greek and Roman, were called saviors. This title often was given to the Greek gods. Other terms that convey the concept of redeemer are *pioneer* and *guide*. The author of Hebrews spoke of the pioneer of our faith (Heb. 12:2). Herein is the image of a trailblazer. The image of a mountain guide is meaningful to me because a guide knows the terrain, has had experience with the kinds of difficulties that arise while mountain climbing, and a guide journeys with the mountain climbers. Who of us does not need a trailblazer, a guide, for our lives? If I showed you a newborn infant and said, "This one will be our guide, our trailblazer through life," how would you respond? Probably, at first, you would just stand with a stunned, glazed gaze on your face. You would conclude, as you regained some composure, that I was out of touch with reality. How could an infant be a guide for life and living? No way could such an announcement be good news. It would throw you off balance.

How do you think the shepherds responded to the message that a savior had been born and that they could find this infant trailblazer in a manger in Bethlehem? The shepherds, along with all other Israelites, had expected and longed for God's expression to come in a unique way, but for that expression to be a helpless baby threw them off balance. The only thing they knew to do was to gaze at the baby. Perhaps they anticipated that this infant would have some unique qualities that would attract attention and cause people to change.

Some strange stories developed around the early life of Jesus. One such story was that, as a small boy, Jesus would make birds out of clay, breathe on them, and they would fly. It was difficult to allow a trailblazing messiah to be a normal infant and child. God's arrival was disturbing because this infant was like any other infant. He had his days and nights mixed up. His swaddling clothes had to be changed. He had to be fed and, if he was not fed, he cried. Good news is announced when God arrives, but the message is never quite like people expect it to be.

Another thing that threw people off balance with the good news of God's arrival was the people to whom the message was announced. The good news was announced to Mary, Joseph, and the shepherds. Mary and Joseph were of peasant stock. Neither of them had positions of authority or places of influence. Many people in the first century expected God to intervene in life, to enter the world, right wrongs, and make justice flow down like a river. Because people had seen what the use of force had done, many concluded that God would intervene by means of a strong political-military leader. King David had been such a leader; therefore, the deliverer they anticipated looked a lot like David. People were longing for and looking for the Messiah, God's human deliverer. In spite of the efforts to which some went to demonstrate that Jesus was related to David's family, there just was not anything royal or regal about the birth of a child in a stable to peasant parents.

Messiah-seekers were off balance again when the good news was announced to shepherds. The shepherding profession had taken a nosedive in the respectability polls. Shepherding was an admirable profession in the embryonic, nomadic days of Israel's development. The best-known Psalm 23 identifies God as the Shepherd of people. However, with the development of a more ordered lifestyle, shepherds became religious outcasts. Shepherds were unable to keep all the ceremonial laws about meticulous hand washing and spending the required amount of time in preparation for worship because of their work with sheep. The shepherds belonged to that multitude of common people who were considered outside the pale of religious respectability. Thus, anything that the shepherds claimed had been announced to them could be regarded with great suspect, if not discounted entirely.

God arrived and announced good news to peasants and shepherds. Regardless of what the content of the message was, it was doubted to be an announcement from God because of the people to whom the message was delivered. The religious leaders were convinced that God would make the announcement of good news to the world through the proper channel, namely through the religious establishment. The expected way for the announcement of good news was for God to give the message to the high priest at Passover. He, in turn, would announce God's message as part of the highest worship season when the multitudes would be gathered for worship. The religious leaders were convinced that God needed to get the message to the most people in the quickest way possible. Surely, the religious grapevine would be the path the message would travel. God arrived and good news was announced, but the religious establishment discounted the message because peasants and shepherds claimed to have received the message.

God's arrival did not happen just a few select times in the past. Certainly, God's arrival in Bethlehem 2000 years ago was neither the first nor the last time God arrived in the world. God arrives every day in our lives. We do not see God. God is not tangible as an infant, nor as an adult for that matter, except in the stranger, the sick, the hungry, the imprisoned, and the naked. The late Southern humorist Grady Nutt told in poetic form about the one nugget he mined from college chemistry and applied his treasure to his understanding of God:

I mined this nugget, though, from that dark hole in
    My academic voyage: "No one has ever seen an atom."
Men have dedicated their lives to explaining something
    no one has ever seen.
The plain fact is all we know about the atom
    we know from what it does.
Oh, brother, can you feel the insight percolate,
    truth effervesce, the wisdom ooze, in that plain fact?
Our knowledge of God is like that . . . we know him
    not because we have seen him, but because of
    what he does and what he is.
Certain atoms get together in a certain way and we call
    them water.
Love, truth, joy, affirmation, peace, long-suffering,
    patience—get together in a certain way, and we call
    them Jesus Christ.[1]

Good news is announced when God arrives. If we are preoccupied with how God must come and who must be God's messengers, then the chances are great we will miss the good news. Were it not for Luke, there would be no shepherds, no manger, no stable, and no swaddling clothes in the incarnation story. All of those items were ways for Luke to say there is no one to whom God does not come, and there is no one incapable of being a messenger who announces good news to the poor, sets the captives free, and liberates the oppressed. What about you? Are you caught off balance when God arrives and announces good news?

THANKSGIVING IS OFFERED

I have given thought for some time to designing my own Christmas card. On the outside would be two words in large print, GET LOST. This double meaning statement could be sent to friends and foes alike. On the inside of the card would be the phrase "In Wonder, Love, and Praise." The phrase "lost in wonder, love, and praise" comes from Charles Wesley's beautiful hymn and summarizes what happens to the person who is able to receive the good news when God arrives. This person gets lost in wonder, love, and praise.

Someone has said there are three classes of people: those who make things happen; those who watch things happen; and the overwhelming majority who has no idea what is happening. Each of us is a member of each group at different times, perhaps even at different times during the same day. Philosophically, we may be members of each group as we try to comprehend what it means for God to arrive in our lives. As we contemplate God coming to us, we offer thanksgiving as we get lost in wonder, love, and praise.

How do we get lost in wonder? We live in an informational, technological age in which more is known, understood, and explained about our universe than any of us can comprehend. There is the irony. Even the scientific explanation of how the universe functions gives cause for wonder because the measure of our minds cannot encompass the vastness of the universe. The more we know, the more there is to know, and we are captured by a touch of wonder. Arthur Gordon says that the theme of his book *A Touch of Wonder* is: "It's just a book that reflects one man's ways of looking at things . . . almost always there's a lot more to these commonplace happenings than meets the casual eye . . . and that most people would find a lot more in them if only they would pause and look and feel and care just a bit more than they do."[2] Does the Christ-event call for us to look and feel and care a bit more than we do?

We struggle with the meaning of God coming in Jesus of Nazareth. From the early days of the church, the claim has been made that Jesus was human and divine. Errors have been made in emphasizing one to the exclusion of the other. The Docetic heresy developed. This heresy said that Jesus just appeared to be a man. On the other end of the spectrum were those who saw Jesus as a man only. Jesus really is what God means by a human being, and he is what we mean when we talk about what God is like. Therein are wonder, mystery, and difficulty.

We often state the misconception that seeing is believing. Much of our believing has nothing to do with seeing. Every scientist believes there are atoms, but no scientist has ever seen an atom. The scientist's belief is not based on seeing. What about you as you read these words? Do you believe there are light waves coming at you from every angle? You don't see them, and yet you believe they are present. Many of us watch television. This activity says that we believe there are light and sound waves in our homes although we have never seen them. We turn on our television sets and right before our eyes and ears the light and sound waves are taken out of the atmosphere and transmitted into visible images we can see and audible sounds we can hear and understand.

The existence of Jesus of Nazareth as both human and divine is mystery and wonder. Jesus took that which was beyond human capacities to comprehend and transmitted it into images that people could see and sounds they could hear. Thus, the more we learn and know about Jesus, the more we learn and know about God and about what it means to be an authentic human being. When God arrives, we need to get lost in wonder.

Much of the world of the first century lived in expectation of a world redeemer, and many Jews expected a messiah. There were Eastern Magi (wise men) or soothsayers who variously were considered as magicians, astrologers, or sages. The Magi were skilled in philosophy, medicine, and natural science. These men were good people who sought truth. Only later did the practice degenerate into magical contortions and religious sideshows. Astrology was very popular in the first century. People believed that the future could be determined from the placement of the stars. Many people in the first century believed that the star under which one was born settled a person's destiny.

A star was important in Luke's account of the birth of Jesus. Perhaps you have noticed there are differences in the Gospel accounts of Jesus' birth. Only Luke tells about Joseph and Mary's residence in Nazareth. Only Matthew tells about the visit of the Magi and the two-year sojourn in Egypt. Regardless of the facts that the Gospel writers include or omit, all of them wrote for the same purpose. They wrote about the life of Jesus to illustrate and demonstrate the love of God for all humankind.

Leslie Weatherhead was an air raid warden during the awful days of the London blitz of World War II. He told of making his rounds one night after an unusually heavy attack and happening upon an eight-year-old boy who sat sobbing amid the smoking ruins. Weatherhead asked if he had gotten lost, and he nodded affirmatively. Then he asked, "Where does your father live?"

The boy responded, "He's overseas in the service."

"What about your mother and brothers and sisters?"

"I don't have any. They've all been killed," was his reply.

"Do you have any other family—uncles, aunts, grandparents?"

The boy shook his head, "No."

Weatherhead stooped down near the child's face and asked, "Son, who are you?" And with that the boy began to sob compulsively and said, "Mister, I ain't nobody's nothing." Spiritually speaking, there is a world of people who regard themselves as utter orphans in an empty universe. They feel like motherless, fatherless children—nobody's nothings.

I attended a conference several years ago where I heard Linda Long of *Sesame Street* interviewed. During the interview, Linda recalled a significant event from her childhood. She grew up in the Midwest. Her family was economically deprived. One day she was on the dusty porch with her mother looking out over the prairie and Linda said to her mother, "You know, Mom, someday I'm gonna be somebody." Her mother reached down, lifted Linda up in her arms and said, "Linda, you are somebody now."

The Creator, Redeemer, and Sustainer of the universe became flesh and blood in Jesus of Nazareth as a way to embrace us and say, "You are somebody now." What happens to us makes a difference to God.

Karl Barth, the great German theologian, wrote some monumental volumes covering all aspects of the life and teachings of Christ. He was asked during a question-and-answer period following a lecture at a German university, "What is the most profound truth you have discovered in your theological studies?" Without pausing a moment, the noted theologian said, "Jesus loves me, this I know, for the Bible tells me so." I encourage you to get lost in the love of God because you are somebody now.

Being somebody often is experienced at Christmas. People who are forgotten are remembered at Christmas. Children who receive little attention from a parent during the rest of the year are remembered at Christmas. The hope of being somebody is sparked.

Unfortunately, though, while many things occur during the Christmas season to affirm that we are somebody, the same season often exposes us at our worst. We are seen rushing here and there to grab gifts, wrapping paper, fruit, and nuts. We rush in to church in an attempt to keep some sanity about us and about the purpose of the season. One Christmas season as I was hurrying with my shopping, I saw a shopper grab the last Simon toy and saw the disappointment in the face of another who, with shorter arms, was reaching for the same toy. Abraham Lincoln said something that could illustrate this scene when he said that the quarreling and arguing his sons were doing was a symbol of the world: "I have three English walnuts and each boy wants two."

The Christmas season so often epitomizes our whole approach to life. We are eager to see what we can get and seldom consider what we can give. Matthew wrote something significant about the magi in his account of Jesus' birth. He said they brought gifts, knelt down, and worshiped him (Mt. 2:11). They made a tangible response by bringing gifts. There is a sense that how we act at Christmas reveals how we are at our best. What does that say about us? What we need is to be converted, changed, and turned in another direction.

Dr. Seuss wrote about this kind of conversion in *How the Grinch Stole Christmas*. The Grinch had great hostility toward the people of Who-Ville. They all seemed so joyous at Christmas. The people were clattering and clamoring about giving and receiving gifts. In his anger, the Grinch stole the gifts, decorations, trees, and food only to discover that Christmas was more than these were. The Grinch's problem was that his heart was two sizes too small. When his heart grew three sizes, the Grinch returned the trappings of Christmas to Who-Ville and joined the celebration. Our hearts are two sizes too small. We need to be converted from "What will I get?" to "What will I give?" and discover our hearts growing three sizes.

The best gifts are not those that are purchased at the most expensive stores. Actually, they aren't those that are purchased at all. Often, they are what seemed at the time to be insignificant encounters or events within relationships. Having worked with several people who were dying and having talked with numerous colleagues engaged in the same work, memories of interaction with a child or a tender moment shared with a friend are most significant. These are the things that energize and encourage people and give meaning to their lives.

Relationships are of authentic significance to human beings. What we need is to offer thanks to God for the gift of life that has come to us and for the meaning of life that comes because God comes to us. Like the Magi, we need to bring gifts, namely ourselves, and offer them to God so that we might get lost in praise of God.

When God arrives in the world, and God is always present and constantly arriving simultaneously, life continues as usual. Before very long when God arrives, fear arises, and then good news is announced. Once we have gotten our balance back after hearing the good news, we can offer thanks to God. We get lost in wonder, love, and praise when gratitude to God permeates our lives. Then we catch a glimpse of what it means for God to come to the world with love.

QUESTIONS TO PONDER

1. Reflect on times in your life when God arrived and your life continued as usual. Why?

2. What babies have influenced your life? Why? How?

3. What is frightening about God arriving in your life?

4. How has God's good news thrown you off balance?

5. What causes you to offer thanks?

6. For what are you most grateful in your life? Why?

7. How do you know that God has arrived in your life?

2

WHAT IS GOD DOING IN THE WORLD?

Isaiah 40:12–31

"What is God doing in the world?" is a question we have asked in a variety of ways. Often a tone of cynicism betrays our conviction that God is doing nothing. On other occasions, we are convinced that God ought to have nothing to do with the world. The biblical record and the experiences of our religious ancestors tell us that God has been actively engaged in and with the world from the beginning of the creation (Gen. 1:1). God has not and will not abandon the world (Isa. 41:17).

We human beings have the ability to relate to God, the unseen and ultimate of life. This is part of our capacity because we are created in the image of God. Nevertheless, there are many occasions when we need the presence of God to be revealed in and through a fellow human being, someone with a skin face. Theologian Reinhold Niebuhr is credited with saying, "Nothing is ever real until it is local." How true this is of our encounters with God! God becomes real as we encounter God in a fellow human being.

As God engages us, seldom is the encounter engulfed with fanfare and fireworks. Rather, softly, quietly, we experience God, and only later, as we reflect on the event, do our lives shake or our bodies tremble as we realize we have been in the presence of the living God.

God encounters people. But the question raised repeatedly is, "What is God doing in the world?" God is bringing hope, peace, love, and joy to the world.

BRINGING HOPE

Erik Erikson, an authority on human development, emphasized that hope is a basic necessity of life if life is to be purposeful and filled with meaning. Hope is the confident assurance that provides us with vision. The author of Proverbs (29:18) understood correctly that people without vision perish.

WHAT IS GOD DOING IN THE WORLD?

There is a direct correlation between the source of our hope and the vision we have. A young lad in the Mell Lazarus comic strip "Miss Peach" told Miss Peach that what frightened him most about life was, "Realizing that my future is in the hands of a hopelessly incompetent fool, namely me!" The lad saw himself as the source of his hope. That was a hopeless vision.

Hope is the compass of life that gives direction to our living. It is the power of the future to shape the present. The summer before I entered college, I engaged in a rigorous running program to get into good physical condition in hope of getting a basketball scholarship. Near the end of the summer, I lost hope of receiving one. I stopped running halfway through my workout and walked home. I have never used running as a regular form of exercise since then. What I hoped for in the future made me a different person in the present.

Hope is that unproved conviction that both life and death have genuine meaning. Hope is the power and willingness to take risks even when all of life is uncertain. Hope is the ability to make decisions related to open-ended situations believing that even through the risks we are growing, living, and finding purpose in our existence.

In a sense, hope refers to the future, that part beyond us that someone else might place at our disposal. Marriage is an illustration. Marriage is built on the future that two people place at each other's disposal and, in essence, say to each other: "All the future that may be out before us, we will face together." In this situation, hope becomes the expectation of the future of the other based on the conviction that what one has promised, one intends to do.

The catchword in the writings of the prophets and the apostles about any hopeful event is *new*. The Hebrew Scriptures speak of the New Exodus, the New Conquest, the New Zion, the New Covenant, the New Life, and the New Commandments. God was the source of hope for the people, and the hope found expression in the new.

Hope is kindled in the tension between the old and the new. Each of us has felt the heat sparked by the old and the new rubbing together. The heat is felt keenly in homes where teenagers are maturing. The sparks fly as they develop some independence from Mom and Dad. Yet there is evidence of hope in the tension between the old and the new. Hope is kindled as the discovery is made that new can grow out of the old. Hope is making monuments out of rubble, whistling your way to renewal, bouncing off walls but bouncing up. Grady Nutt defined hope as the trademark of confidence, the fuel of achievement.[1] It reaches out for the future with open expectation to what it might bring. Hope forsakes the old and the inadequate both inwardly and outwardly as it looks toward something new.

Every generation is thrashed by the tidal wave of change. Change is inevitable and frightening. There are times in our lives when everything we had nailed down seems to be coming loose. When life is in such a state of flux, we scramble for security. It is not unusual for people to cry out in the face of threatening change, "Give me that old-time religion." They are much like the woman who opposed putting stained-glass windows in the new church building because she preferred the glass "just as God made it." Both glass and religion are made out of elements supplied by God, but neither comes directly from the hand of the Almighty.

The cry for old-time religion is a delusion and an evasion. The main difficulty with the desire for old-time religion is that it is seldom old enough. Usually the people crying for old-time religion are referring to their perception of how things were thirty or forty years earlier in their lives when, as they remember, things were a lot simpler. Old-time religion, in order to be old enough, needs to go back at least to Abraham. Abraham left his homeland in Ur of the Chaldeans and went out not knowing where he was going. Abraham had hope because he allowed the future to shape the present in his life. Old-time religion is pioneering for God into new fields and new days. Old-time religion calls for pilgrims, like Abraham, who will get out of familiar and comfortable ruts of custom, who will get out of smug little dogmatisms. Many prefer to choose the way of Cain rather than the way of Abraham. Cain lived in the land of Nod, which means wanderer. Abraham was a pilgrim; Cain was a wanderer. Hope is what distinguishes a pilgrim from a wanderer. Hope is what enables people to get up from whatever crashes their ship, to get out of their life jackets, and to swim out. Each time they learn something new and become better people. Every time they are able to begin again. Often we are frozen by fear, the fear that what happens to us in life will break us rather than reshape us.

This is why we need hope to be our compass in life. There are times when our journey becomes an endless sea and we may lose our way on the high sea of life. We will come to the hope of finding our way to shore or we will come to despair when this happens. Despair means "to lose breath." Philosopher Sören Kierkegaard said that despair is the sickness that leads to death. Hope is a part of giving inspiration or new breath to finding our way.

Thus, there are two sailors on the sea, one who has despair of finding her way and the other who has hope. Both are at the same spot but in very different places. The despairer is getting near the end; the hopeful person is on the verge of a whole new experience. The despairer, like Cain, becomes the wanderer with life running out of zest. The hopeful person, like Abraham, is the pilgrim who has a source for renewal.

What is the source for this hope? In what is hope grounded? If our hope rests with us, then our future is in the hands of hopelessly incompetent fools, namely, us! Hope is the underlying theme of scripture. It is a basic premise of existence from the biblical perspective. Hope is the expectation of what is positive, closely connected with confidence, eagerly on the lookout, patiently waiting, or seeking refuge. Hope is always expecting something positive and it is centered in God. Especially in the Hebrew Scriptures, less is said about what is hoped for than about the reason for hoping—God and a relationship with God. Salvation often is described as a time of confidence. Thus, for Jeremiah (29:11) and Hosea (6:2–3), God grants hope instead of help, and of course, hope is the very help that both prophets needed.

The psalmist had a beautiful analogy of hope. He said that he waited upon God "more than watchmen for the morning" (Ps.130:6 RSV). The watchman waits for the dawn with confidence that the dawn will come. What watchman ever waited believing the dawn would not arrive! This is the kind of hope the psalmist had in God because God was the source of his hope.

Isaiah 40:12–31 is one of the most beautiful passages in all of scripture. It is marked with beauty by the way it portrays God bringing hope to people. The Babylonian Exile is the historical backdrop for this passage. Describing the sky as a curtain and a tent in which God dwells, the prophet is like a skilled photographer projecting word pictures on the minds of his listeners. The prophetic artist, using words as his paint, makes broad strokes to portray the backdrop of creation in front of which and against which he brings into focus his stirring imagery of hope in these words: "But they who wait for the Lord shall renew their strength, they shall mount up with wings like eagles, they shall run and not be weary, they shall walk and not faint" (Isa. 40:31 RSV).

Many of the Israelites had become disillusioned and disappointed as a result of being in exile. They never thought such devastation could happen to them. They equated their circumstances with the action or lack of action by God. Many of them were about to switch sides in the middle of a severe crisis. At that point, the prophet delivered his beautiful and hopeful message.

Isaiah's word of hope to the Israelites in exile is a word of hope to us in our exiles. There are many exile events that affect our lives. Accidents, disease, debilitating illness, broken relationships, death, and personal and internal conflict are only a few of the crises that may overtake us and carry us off captives and victims instead of allowing us to be captors and victors. We are either entering or exiting from some exilic encounter in our lives nearly every day. We cry out in a variety of ways the unison message, "What is God doing in the world?" Isaiah's answer is that God is bringing hope.

Isaiah said that those who wait on the Lord will receive renewed strength. Waiting on the Lord does not mean to sit passively and accept whatever comes as a handout from God. Such an approach has much to do with fate and nothing to do with faith. To wait on the Lord does not mean whatever will be, will be.

Perhaps the work of farmers is the best analogy to define what it means to wait upon the Lord. Anticipation is part of farmers' work. First, they anticipate the spring thaw and the drying of the soil. Then they cultivate the land by plowing and disking. Next they enrich the soil with lime and fertilizer.

Then they plant the seed, let's say, corn. They anticipate the sun and the rain to cause the corn to grow. As the plants push through the soil and begin to grow, farmers plow between the rows to keep out the weeds and enable the corn to grow stronger. They anticipate the coming harvest. When the blade has developed, the ear grows, and finally the grain. Then, at the right time, the farmers harvest the corn. The farmers have spent approximately six months waiting to harvest the corn crop, waiting in the sense of eagerly anticipating it and being actively involved in its development.

Isaiah said that renewed strength would come to those who eagerly anticipated the coming of God to their lives and who were actively interacting with God. The author said that the assurance of God might take the form of ecstasy, activism, or walking. We need to realize that the forms of God's hope and help are many. The particular vision of God we take into the shadows that are cast upon our lives is also important.

Whatever form exile may take for us, ecstasy may result from our eager anticipation of the deliverance of God. God's presence can bring hope and strength in such a way that we soar like an eagle into an atmosphere of sheer exuberance. I have had a few such encounters. I must admit that I have met more people who have claimed ecstatic experiences from God than I have experienced personally. Perhaps you have known those moments of exhilarating joy and celebration that were the result of your encounter with God. Yet, if we conclude that this is the only way God gives us strength and hope, then we will be greatly disappointed in the midst of the kind of darkness that often engulfs us.

Part of my work is ministering to people who are grief stricken because of the breakup of their family or the death of an important person in their lives. There is no ecstasy in these experiences. No one is overcome with joy in the midst of such sorrow. There are moments in the depths of human suffering when the soaring of ecstasy would be out of touch with reality. If this is the only form of expectation—the only shape of God's hope that we can acknowledge—then we are sure to feel betrayed and disappointed in the shadows of life.

Isaiah said that a second way of responding to God bringing hope was to run and not be weary. This is a response of activism. This is the inspiration to do a job, to get on with a task. Often there is a spark within us to do something. Our religious convictions have motivated us and empowered us to get busy with a project, to become involved in an endeavor, to cease sitting on the sidelines. But, once again, if this is our only view of the result of God bringing hope, then we will be frustrated and disappointed. Few of us function very well in situations in which we feel helpless. A person is dying. We cannot prevent his death. We pray. We obtain the best possible medical assistance. But there is no way that we can run and not be weary.

There is yet a third response to the hope that God brings: "They shall walk and not faint." There really is nothing spectacular about this response. After all, if we were given three choices, who of us would not prefer flying or running to walking? There was a time in my life when one of my weekly responsibilities was sermon preparation. Every week I hoped the preparation would soar or at least develop at a running pace, but invariably the sermon developed at a snail's pace. For me, in this time of preparation, "to walk and not faint" was the most I could possibly do. And so it is in the crises of life with which you and I must deal and to which we must respond.

Life has its dark stretches. The most difficult discipline in the midst of them is not that of flying or running. Rather, it is keeping on keeping on when the heavy struggles of life have slowed us to a walk and when it seems, in spite of everything, we are going to faint under the load. Isaiah said that God brings hope to the world and to those of us in the world. The worst that God's hope can do is to give us the strength to walk and not faint. Is that not enough? What more do we need?

BRINGING PEACE

The world is in a turbulent state. Tensions escalate between nations. Relationships between the United States and other nations fluctuate. Wars continue to rage in various part of the world. Who knows where the tension will erupt into war and destruction next? It is in this context that our cynicism is clearly communicated when we ask, "What is God doing in the world?" To respond that God is bringing peace is to risk either being considered out of touch with reality or laughed into obscurity.

Micah 4:1–7 offers some challenging words for us. He said that the Lord would teach us what to do. God will settle disputes among nations and gather people to make a new beginning. But this raises questions. Will we be open to learn from God the things that make for peace? Are we teachable or have we made up our minds that there is nothing new under the sun for us?

What is this peace that God is bringing into the world? It is more than an absence of war. Supposedly we have that now. Candidates for national office in the United States enjoy boasting about the peacetime in which we live. It may be peacetime, but life is not peaceful. We continue near the brink of nuclear holocaust and hover under the nuclear cloud.

The literature of civilization is filled with compositions that express longings for peace. The biblical words for peace are powerful, expansive, and inclusive. *Shalom* is the Hebrew and *eirene* is the Greek. Both words mean that everything is working for the highest good for a person. The words gather up all the positive aspirations of the human quest—wholeness, completeness, fulfillment, well-being, satisfaction, and joy.

We need to encounter the God of peace and the peace of God. It is in and through these encounters that we are able to receive this gift of peace that God brings. The peace of God passes all understanding and comes to us through human beings. The divine encounter comes through the human encounter. Anticipation of this encounter is almost as significant as the encounter itself. The Advent season developed in Christianity many centuries ago as a season of expectation and preparation for Christmas. Advent continues to be a season of preparation and expectation for many Christians as they anticipate God coming to them in new ways.

God is seeking to come to us and bring us peace. God comes to us today like God has come in the past. God came in Abraham's unrest, in Jacob's dream, in Moses' solitude, in Ruth's grief, in Mary's pregnancy, to shepherds and wise men through stables and stars, to Mary Magdalene through acceptance, to Zacchaeus through lunch, to Nicodemus by night, to the Ethiopian eunuch through conversation with Philip. God comes to you and me through gradual awareness—first a dim light in the distance like the breaking of dawn and then, at times, as bright as the noonday sun. As God comes, peace is brought. This is what God is doing in the world.

Peace, like any gift, requires recipients. It is the nature of a gift that it is to be received. Tension is created when a gift is offered. The one who receives a gift feels the tug between dependence and independence. It may not be easy to receive a gift without feeling some obligation and indebtedness to the giver. Have you received a gift from someone for whom you did not have a gift? Did you feel some obligation to give that person a gift in return? Of course, there are a few donors who give gifts and never let the recipients forget that they have been the recipients of gifts.

Peace is a gift that God brings to the world. This gift is offered with the possibility of being rejected. If the gift of God's peace is received, it changes people's lives from the inside out so that their very nature and attitude are altered toward reconciliation. Micah spoke about this peace. Peace for Micah meant the state of wholeness possessed by individuals or groups of people. The characteristics of this wholeness included health, prosperity, and security as a result of spiritual completeness of the covenant relationship with God. How far from this understanding our thoughts of peace are! Usually, peace for us means the ability to pursue the ordinary rounds of life without interruption and without struggle. When life does not go smoothly for us, we are heard shouting disturbingly, "Give me a little peace and quiet!"

I suspect that you want peace in your private life and in our public world. But how have you resisted God's peace? The peace of God that passes all understanding causes its own kind of turbulence. The peace of God was embodied in the Prince of Peace. Yet, one of the paradoxes of his life was that he knew trouble wherever he went. The gift of peace he offered was so radical that the people who received this gift often found their lives uprooted. Some of them held on even more tenaciously. The gift of peace that Christ offered involved reconciliation between God and people. Such reconciliation required a switching of loyalties. A certain amount of turmoil will occur when some loyalties are thawing and others are being formed. Jesus described this as a process of bringing a sword rather than peace. Surgery often is necessary for healing and wholeness, but it causes pain, hurt, and illness before the peace of health comes. Many who undergo surgery feel worse for a while after surgery than they did prior to the surgery. The gift of peace that God brings to us often makes us feel worse before it helps us feel better because it involves a switching of loyalties. We feel insecure and unsure as we switch loyalties.

Biblical religion portrays God seeking to give peace to the creation. Only in this religion do we have a God who weeps for creation. The gods in other religions are portrayed as uninvolved and disinterested in what happens to their domains or as wreaking havoc upon the world as the mood strikes them. But in biblical faith, what God did in the world was to pour as much of God into Jesus of Nazareth as was possible to pour into one person. Later, this one who became the presence of God in human flesh crested the hill overlooking Jerusalem and began to sob, "Would that even today you knew the things that make for peace!" (Lk. 19:42 RSV).

God lives with the disappointment of wanting something for us that we may not want for ourselves. God always has been more committed to the goal of bringing peace than people have been. Jesus was neither giving up in despair nor blowing up in rage as he approached Jerusalem. He was shedding real tears for the folly and fate of Jerusalem. He had offered, and continued to offer, the gift of peace, but they would not receive the gift.

Jesus put his finger on one of our basic problems as human beings. We do not know the things that make for peace. A civil war rages in each of us. Like Peter, we have very little peace in ourselves so all that it takes is a tiny provocation to set our warlike forces into motion. Like Paul, we do the evil that we claim we do not want to do and neglect the good that we claim is our desire to do.

We are contradictory when we talk about peace but use violence to resolve conflict. Hitting and physical fighting are the ways used to resolve differences and conflict in more homes than any of us really want to admit. Parents hit their children; husbands hit wives; wives hit husbands; siblings hit each other; neighbors fight neighbors. It is a sobering fact that the family is the most violent institution in the United States. Violence leads to more violence. Mahatma Gandhi said "the means are the ends at an incipient stage." The kind of consequences we are going to produce is already embedded in the means we employ. We need to remember this as people seek to persuade us that violent means are the way to create a peaceful end. Jesus countered the eye for an eye of his ancestors. Gandhi worded it well when he said that if everybody acted upon the instruction of an eye for an eye and a tooth for a tooth, all of us would be blind and toothless.

Too often we are heard asking the wrong question, "When will God come into the world bringing peace?" The question we need to be asking is, "When will we permit God to bring peace into our lives?" God comes to the world in and through the peacemakers. They are the pacesetters of life. Jesus said, "Happy are the peacemakers for they shall be called the children of God" (Mt. 5:9 AT). Peacemakers are happy not because they spread cheer, but because they create peace where there is hatred, they reconcile where there is separation. These are the children of God who draw upon the peace they have received from God. The price of this peace is expensive in terms of external unrest, discomfort, abuse, and the threat of destruction.

Jesus was a peacemaker and his life revealed what happens when God comes in peace. Jesus was surrounded by contradictions, conflicts, and conspiracies. The Prince of Peace found no peace for himself on earth. Wherever Jesus went, trouble followed. He stood against the full force of evil. He was hated by the authorities and ruling classes, misunderstood by the masses, deserted by his friends. He was surrounded by trouble until the waves of calamity submerged him completely. It became evident that there was a unity between the Spirit of God and the spirit of humanity that remained beyond tragedy and survived all the accidents of life and death only after the deadliest thing had happened.

Peacemakers are the children of God. The life of a peacemaker is risky, unsettling, and difficult. It is more difficult to work for peace and reconciliation than to work toward conflict, unrest, and war. Peacemakers place themselves in precarious and potentially destructive positions. By the very nature of their approaches, peacemakers become extremely vulnerable to those who refuse to have anything to do with peace.

My great-great-great-grandfather was affectionately known throughout Wayne County, Kentucky, as Uncle Billy Cooper. He was a Baptist preacher in that county during the Civil War. The heat of the war ignited his fellow citizens into a white-heated frenzy. In their grandiosity, the citizens decided to pass out guns, choose up sides, and settle the Civil War on the streets of Monticello. It was Uncle Billy Cooper who stood between the Blue and the Gray and pleaded with them to put down their destructive weapons and their destructive attitudes. At the risk of being blown away by both sides simultaneously, Uncle Billy Cooper sought to bring peace and reconciliation to a community that was ready to tear itself apart. Why would a person attempt such a foolish thing? Because he believed God would teach people what they needed to know. Because he believed God was bringing peace to the world. Because he believed that God had the power and the desire to settle disputes within a nation as well as among nations. Because he believed that children of God are peacemakers. Because he believed that when people become peacemakers, no one can make them afraid.

What is God doing in the world? God is bringing peace. Peace is God's gift to us, but it must be received in order to be experienced. For God to come in peace to us means we will beat our destructive attitudes into constructive relationships. Are we willing to be that radical?

BRINGING LOVE

We always need to hear a word from God. In hearing a word from God, we need to discover *the* Word of God. There are so many words. The Bible contains thousands of words. Millions of words have been used to interpret the thousands of biblical words. In our verbosity, we often hide ourselves behind the screen of words we use. Too often we are speaking but saying nothing, expounding but proclaiming little. Our words become sounding brass and tinkling cymbals.

What is *the* Word of God in all of this? All the words about God can be reduced to one word: *love*. All the messages from God to humanity are knit together by one message: *love*. God's activity in history reveals one proclamation: God is LOVE! *The* Word of God is *love*. What is God doing in the world? God is bringing love to the world. God comes into the world bringing hope, peace, and joy because God is love.

The Advent-Christmas season of the Christian year is when the love of God is highlighted more than any other time. This season signifies the desire of God to get the message through to us. As much of God as could be in a human being was poured into Jesus of Nazareth so that we could see and feel God's love in flesh and blood. The Advent season is a time for Christians to celebrate with pageantry what always has been true of God—that God is love and always has sought to come to the world in love. What happened the first Christmas was not a new approach by God, just a manifestation of God reaching out to creation. God's coming to us today is not a new approach, just a continuation of the way God always has sought to come to the world.

The Word of God is love and it is written all over biblical religion. Love is imprinted in the Garden of Eden. It underscored the Exodus and the wilderness wanderings. It is etched in the Ten Commandments. It is echoed in the messages of the prophets.

Jesus was empowered by this love of God and he sought to express the love that flowed through him in a variety of ways to benefit others. He used his love to rescue people from entrapments into which they had gotten themselves. There were many risks involved in Jesus doing this. One such risk was to foster a perpetual relationship of dependency of rescuer and rescuee. Jesus did not want to establish a permanent relationship of dependency of one human being upon another. Thus, he taught, "Call no man your father" (Mt. 23:9 RSV). No human being can meet all of the needs and expectations of another human being or solve all of another's problems.

The premise of Sheldon Kopp's book, *If You Meet the Buddha on the Road, Kill Him*, speaks to this point. Kopp wrote that if you entertain the idea that someone can do everything you need done, then the wisest thing to do is to kill that illusion immediately.

No one is strong enough always to be the rescuer. No one is weak enough always to need to be rescued. Our dependency needs to be on God whose creative love can redeem us. When God's love is joined with our strength, we are empowered to love others as God loves us.

The fairy tale "Beauty and the Beast" illustrates the potency that love has. As the story goes, there was a poor man who was so hungry that he resorted to stealing from the castle garden. He was caught by an ugly creature who had the head of an animal and the body of a man. The Beast threatened to put the man in the dungeon unless he would allow his younger daughter, Beauty, to come and live in the castle. The man went home and explained the situation to his family, and Beauty agreed to the sentence. As soon as Beauty was in the castle, the Beast fell in love with her and began asking her to marry him. He treated her kindly, but she could not bring herself close to him because of his grotesque appearance. The Beast became sadder and sadder as if he were going to die. The Beast made one last proposal and Beauty had a change of heart. She professed that she did love him. She embraced the Beast and kissed him. Instantly, the Beast was transformed into a handsome prince. Much earlier in life, he had been put under the curse of an evil witch and doomed to a grotesque form until someone would love him in spite of his ugliness.

Love is a creative power in a world of ugliness. Who of us is worthy of the love of God when we assess our lives from God's perspective? But love is a gift and gifts are to be received. They cannot be earned. Love for another, regardless of what it costs the one loving, is what John called perfect love (1 Jn. 4:18). Perfect love casts out fear. Fear paralyzes and inhibits human efforts. It separates individuals from one another and creates between them an atmosphere of suspicion. Fear creates conditions that encourage violence. Fear causes emotional and mental illness in individuals and groups and impedes growth toward maturity. Fear often causes us to choose beast-like methods to deal with beastly characteristics. "Fight fire with fire," we say. The net effect when a person answers evil with evil and gives badness a dose of its own medicine is an increase of evil and an expansion of the original problem. The only real solution to evil is to overcome evil with good. What goodness can do to evil is far greater than what evil can do to goodness. Love counts not the cost. A reporter was watching a Catholic nun mop the gangrenous wounds of a Chinese soldier. "I wouldn't do that for a million dollars," said the reporter. "Neither would I," the nun replied and went on mopping.

English historian Edward Gibbon's *The History of the Decline and Fall of the Roman Empire* indicates how the gladiatorial games came to an end in the fifth century C.E. Thousands of people filled the coliseum to enjoy watching gladiators fighting each other to death. A monk who lived in the desert came to Rome and followed the flow of the crowd into the coliseum. He saw what was happening, entered the ring, and separated the gladiators. At first the crowd laughed at the comedy—then, angry and incensed, they started throwing rocks and stoned the monk to death. Their brutality stood out in bold relief as they saw the monk's corpse lying there. According to Gibbon, the stands emptied and there was never again a gladiatorial combat in Rome. The act of remaining humane had a redeeming impact on those causing the evil. The curse of evil was broken when someone unlovable was given the gift of love. A better way of life has been visible in history since the days of Abraham when people began to connect their strength to the love of God.

The evidence surrounds us that we are in love with ourselves. God is not popular. We vote against God every day. Fortunately, God's position does not depend on popular vote. God has every right to respond, "I can't believe you are doing this to me after all I have done for you." There is no indication anywhere that this is God's response. Apparently, God is willing to take what few people there are who will accept God's love and commit themselves to be partners with God.

The prophets called this handful of respondents "the remnant." A remnant is what is left over. How different we are from God! A lot of people will have nothing to do with leftovers. Not so with God. God's people are the leftovers. The prophets knew that God was trying desperately to do something for the world. God wants to take the lives that people have broken into bits and make them whole again. It is a costly endeavor, but this is what God is doing in the world.

God is love and God asks us to love in return. This is the costliest thing that has been said about God and it is the costliest thing that can be said about us. It is God bringing love to the world and asking us to love the world that is so offensive about the gospel and its persistent upsetting of religious applecarts. Some shabbily dressed street person walks into our lives and says through blurry eyes, "Love me." That is upsetting. Some dependent person tries to grab some of our time. A lonely person telephones at mealtime and wants to talk. It is just one interruption after another. Maybe that is why Mark Twain said that what troubled him most about the Bible was not what he failed to understand, but what he understood quite clearly and could not stomach.

The Bible is clear that the power of God is the redeeming, creative love that is a gift, and when it is received, the light goes on for the one who receives the gift of God's love. Love involves a commitment that has no guarantee. God has taken this kind of risk with us. Often we claim we are afraid of not being loved, but the deeper reality may be that we are afraid of loving. God's kind of love shows us how much there is in the world that is all wrong. God's will drives us across the frontier of a strange country. It is the kind of caring that refuses to let us rest in a place where there is so little the way Christ wants it. There is no promise at all of the static stance that comes with having most things as we want them.

What is God doing in the world? God is caring enough to give the very best. God wrapped love in human flesh and dwelt among people with human flesh. God asks us to be representatives in the flesh today of this same love. God is love and God is seeking to love the world through us. God is bringing love to the world.

BRINGING JOY

Joy is as elusive as a butterfly. Once you think you have caught it, it escapes you. Joy is a by-product of life. God is bringing joy to us as a by-product of bringing us hope, peace, and love. Often joy eludes us because we think we can find it and capture it. We look for joy much like we hunt for snipes.

One of the fun events of a teenage summer camp experience was taking a fellow camper snipe hunting. We waited until late at night, which, as you know, is the best time to catch snipes. We found a good location for this young man. We placed him in the most advantageous position. We gave him a paper bag and a flashlight and left him. When we returned two hours later, he was still holding the bag and the light, but he had failed to catch any snipes. We often look for joy the same way. We hold our bags full of experiences and the light of a relationship with God and we expect joy to fall on us and engulf us. We fail to realize that joy is a by-product of our encounter with God.

Joy means to be in harmony with life. When people's lives are in harmony, their entire beings function as a complete unit. Their minds, their bodies, their attitudes, and their intentions are congruent. An aircraft engineer who helped build engines said, "The secret of making an effective engine is the degree to which we get harmony into that engine. Stress and resistance must be reduced to the lowest point. The parts of an engine, being component parts of a dynamic universe, all work in harmony, and the engine actually sings for joy."

A beautiful sight to me is seeing people whose lives are harmonious and their lives sing for joy in the manner and attitude by which they live. I work with many people on an individual basis whose lives are torn apart by stress and resistance. Their eyes are windows to their lives. The change reflected in their eyes is amazing as they begin to discover and experience some harmony in their lives. Something great happens when people harmonize their lives with God whereby they are relieved of the conflicts, stresses, and resistances that previously defeated them.

What is the secret that leads people to experience this joy? I think the secret has to do with the ability of people to get outside themselves. The temptation always stares us in the face to take ourselves too seriously. Jesus taught that the way to resist this temptation was for people to get outside themselves by seeking to serve others rather than desiring to be served. The failure of people to get outside themselves results in narrowed vision, self-pity, and self-centeredness.

The wisdom that Jesus offered us is that we become filled with joy when we lose ourselves in something greater than ourselves. Joy is a by-product of our experience when we struggle for something in human welfare, fight for somebody else, work for the underprivileged and the downtrodden, and when we work diligently for the good of others in serving God. We find ourselves singing for joy even though we are in the midst of conflicts.

Arthur Gordon tells about joining three friends at a sea cottage to have lunch on a cold winter's day. The friends were a young couple and a retired college professor. The four of them planned a walk on the beach after lunch, but soon after they had finished, the temperature dropped and the wind began to gust. The young couple decided they would much prefer to stay by the warm fire and watch television rather than to risk getting pneumonia in a sea breeze. The professor went to his car and got an ax. He said there was plenty of driftwood along the beach and that he was going to cut a load of firewood. Gordon questioned the man's sanity, to which the professor replied, "It's better than practicing the deadly art of nonliving, isn't it?"[2]

The professor was right. The tendency of too many of us is to seek to conserve rather than to act, avoid rather than to participate, and be passive rather than aggressive. The tendency is to give in to the sly, negative, cautionary voices that constantly caution us to be careful, to be controlled, to be wary, to be prudent, and to be hesitant and guarded in our approach to the complications of life. Jesus expressed the antidote for the art of nonliving when he said, "These things I have spoken to you, that my joy may be in you, and that your joy may be full" (Jn. 15:11 RSV).

The joy that God brings is the ability to react with eagerness. There are ample times in our lives when we do not react with much, if any, eagerness. I suspect that part of the reason is because we are trapped in ourselves. We fail to look beyond our places and beyond ourselves. There are times when I trap myself in my office with sermon preparation, writing, or counseling and I begin to experience myself practicing the art of nonliving. An antidote for this is to make a visit or two either to the hospital or to someone's home. I come away from such a visit having been ministered to, although my intention was to minister. I think the dynamic at work is that in making such a visit, I am getting outside of myself.

The trouble with many of us is not active, deliberate wickedness, but lethargy. The absence of caring, the lack of involvement in life, the desire to keep our bodies comfortable, well fed, and entertained seems to be all that matters. The more successful we are at this, the more entombed our lives become in solid, immovable flesh. We no longer hear the distant trumpet and go toward it. We say, "When in doubt, don't," and that becomes a motto that keeps us from taking any risks and prevents us from responding with enthusiasm to anyone.

Several years ago, a reporter caught up with Branch Ricky, who had been involved in baseball for over fifty years, and asked him, "What's the greatest thrill you ever got out of baseball?" Ricky's eyes flashed as he answered the question just as quickly as he could, "I haven't had it yet!"

What God is doing in the world is bringing hope, peace, and love. As we receive these gifts, we will discover a fourth gift as a by-product—joy. We will discover that every day is a holiday as we allow God to bring us joy. Holiday means holy day. A holy day is a day set aside because of its specialness. Each day becomes a holy day when God brings joy to us because it is set apart as a day to experience what God is doing in the world.

When this becomes our attitude about living and then anyone asks us, "What is the greatest thrill you have ever had?" we respond naturally, "It hasn't happened yet." Each of us, like Arthur Gordon's professor friend, must be willing, sometimes, to chop wood instead of sit by the fire. God is in the world bringing hope, peace, love, and joy to us and through us to others. To receive the gifts of hope, peace, and love is to discover that the best is yet to be and to experience our joy being made full. What is God doing in the world? God is in the world bringing hope, peace, love, and joy to the world. These gifts are from God and they are ours for the receiving.

QUESTIONS TO PONDER

1. What is the basis of hope in your life?

2. What brings hope to your life?

3. How do you respond when your life is filled with hope?

4. What have you done to make peace?

5. Why does trouble seem to surround those who work for peace?

6. Name three people who have been the "skin face" of God to you.

7. How has God brought joy to your life?

3

THE DRAMA OF GOD COMING
TO THE WORLD

LUKE 1:1 — 2:38

Goethe is credited with the astute observation that the highest cannot be spoken; it can only be acted. Truly, the highest drama is God coming to the world, and it is best portrayed through acting. Words are inadequate to communicate the full impact of what it means for God to become flesh and dwell among people. Children and adults gather every year at Christmas in churches and homes to act out the drama of God coming to the world. And every year it is "the best Christmas pageant ever."[1]

A major ingredient of drama is the building of anticipation fed by expectancy, creating interest and holding attention. Indeed, biblical religion is filled with anticipation fed by expectancy. The Hebrew Scriptures identify people enslaved and point to God as the liberator. Attention is called to oppression, and God is identified as the deliverer. The gospel writers give us the most dramatic expression of God as liberator, deliverer, and redeemer wrapped in human flesh.

Sören Kierkegaard said that worship is a drama in which God is the audience, the congregants are the actors, and the worship leaders are the prompters. I want this chapter to be a drama for you, the reader. As the writer, I will be the prompter. You are the actor, and God is the audience. I will write about the lead characters and the supporting cast in an effort to engage you and me in the drama of God coming to the world.

THE LEAD CHARACTERS

You may never have considered them to be stars in God's drama, but you certainly have identified them as the main characters. Of course, I'm talking about Mary, Joseph, and Jesus. When you were a child and your church did its annual Christmas pageant, you wanted to be one of these characters, didn't you? If you had an infant born just a few weeks before Christmas, you hoped you would be asked to permit your child to be the "baby" Jesus in the Christmas play, didn't you? Let's admit it, we have all secretly dreamed of being the stars in the Christmas drama. I want to focus on the original stars of the drama in the next few pages as a way to help us have a better understanding of them and of ourselves. It is through them and through us that the drama of God coming to the world continues in our generation.

Mary

You may have recently turned on a classical radio station and heard ethereal music that touched an inner core of response and permeated your life. It may have surprised you, if for no other reason than you really do not like classical music. You were unable to understand the words, they were in another language, but there was no doubt that the melodies, instruments, and voices were communicating spirituality at its best.

The music stops and the announcer says you have been listening to the "Magnificat" by Vivaldi or Mozart or Bach. No single passage of scripture is more frequently set to music.

We are not that familiar with the lyrics. We hear them once a year during Advent, but we really have paid little attention to what they communicate. The image that comes to mind is of a dutiful peasant girl, overwhelmed by the presence of an angel, being meekly subservient to God exclaiming: "Behold I am the handmaid of the Lord; let it be to me according to your word" (Lk. 1:38 RSV). We find the statement charming.

But there isn't anything charming in the song that Mary sings. It is a prayerful love song that discloses a great deal about the lovers who turn out to be God and Mary. The love song Mary sings becomes the love song of every oppressed person or group who ever lived. The lyrics identify some terribly disturbing action that God takes on behalf of those who are the oppressed and outcast of society. We middle-of-the-road do-gooders do not hear these lyrics. We filter them out because we do not want to hear that we are going to be brought down while the no-gooders are going to rise and be exalted.

Some understanding of Mary's background may help us hear her love song more clearly. Perhaps for the very first time as we hear her lyrics, we may hear them not only as a prayer, but also as a political expression.[2]

We actually know very little about Mary's family background. She was from the hill country of Galilee and her family lived in the area of Nazareth. She probably was a descendant of the tribe of Levi because Elizabeth, her kinswoman and the mother of John the Baptist, was from the tribe of Levi. The Levitic tribe of Israelites was responsible for providing the ministerial leadership for Israel. They were to own neither land nor herds. They were not to raise any crops. The tithes and offerings from the other tribes were used to support the ministry and worship needs of the Israelites and supply the needs of the Levites. This enabled the Levites to concentrate their energies and abilities on the spiritual leadership and education necessary for the nurture of all Israelites.

Mary was a young woman. One translation identifies her as a girl. One clue about her age is that she was betrothed. Betrothal meant that two people were committed to each other in marriage but they were not yet married. To end a betrothal was the same as getting a divorce. If one of the betrothed died, the other was considered a widow or widower. In her culture, betrothal and marriage occurred very early for a girl. Marriage was understood as the only acceptable way for a woman to be successful, safe, and secure in life. Fathers arranged the marriages of their daughters with responsible men in the community. A common practice was for a father to arrange a marriage for his daughter with a man much older than she because there was clear evidence of the man's responsible nature and the type of livelihood he would provide. Another hint at Mary's youthfulness is the contrast between her and Elizabeth. Luke clearly indicates that Elizabeth had been married a long time and had not given birth to a child. Mary was expecting her first child while she was still identified as a virgin or young maiden. It is likely that Mary was a young teenager at the time of her betrothal to Joseph.

It was to a young girl, perhaps thirteen or fourteen years old, that Gabriel went to deliver a message from God. I am not sure why Gabriel got the nod for this assignment, and there is no indication how Gabriel delivered the message. Did he go in person and knock on Mary's little cottage door and say, "I have good news for you"? Or was the message delivered in a dream, a vision, through Mary's daily waking thoughts, or in the midst of prayer? There are many unanswered questions about this message. In whatever form the message came to Mary, Luke worded it this way: Gabriel said, "Peace be with you! The Lord is with you and has greatly blessed you!" (1:28 TEV). Another translation reads, "Hail, O favored one, the Lord is with you!" (RSV). Why did Gabriel say, "Peace be with you!" Yes, *shalom* was the customary greeting, the normal way to say "Hello" in Hebrew. But I wonder if Gabriel said "Peace" in anticipation of what else he was going to tell Mary, knowing that the message he was delivering would be troubling. Maybe Gabriel said "Peace" to calm himself. After seeing Mary and realizing that the nurture and care of God's son was being entrusted to one so young and naive, maybe it was Gabriel who was most uncomfortable and troubled and most in need of peace.

Mary was immediately troubled by Gabriel's greeting. Why would she have been troubled by Gabriel saying "Hello"? Do you recall someone saying "Hello" to you and you were immediately troubled because of the tone of the messenger's voice or the anxious facial expression? Maybe something nonverbal was communicated from Gabriel to Mary that caused her to feel uncomfortable.

I suspect the cause of Mary's uneasiness was Gabriel's address to her as the favored or blessed of God. Mary may have been troubled because she was about to be asked to do a favor but did not know what the favor was. Or Mary may have been troubled because she knew her history. She knew about some of her ancestors who had been identified as favored or blessed by God and they had not fared so well in life. Moses, Job, Naomi, and Ruth are four. Pick any one of these four and examine their lives. Life became traumatic for them after they got involved with God.

We usually think that being favored or blessed by God results in unbroken pleasure and prosperity. Ease, comfort, and success are equated with the "favor or blessing of God" in many of our minds. This line of reasoning is exploded by the biblical accounts of people who were favored by God. From the biblical perspective, the favor of God is the opportunity to share with God in an important task, to become a partner with God. To be blessed by God is to be invited to participate in the high adventure of redemption that always is a hazardous, difficult, painful journey.

Hardship and suffering became a part of Mary's life as a result of being favored or blessed by God. Mary's life was in order until Gabriel came bringing a message to her from God. She was a young, simple, peasant girl betrothed to a stable, dependable, responsible man. God approached Mary as though out of nowhere, and everything Mary held dear was threatened: her honor, her reputation, her hopes and dreams for the future. Everything that had seemed of worth to Mary was about to be shattered. Shadows began to fall across Mary's life because she was favored of God. Gabriel said "Hello," and Mary's life began to fall apart. She was afraid. Encountering the revelation of God often is disturbing to the point of fear. The effect of God being revealed to a person may be overwhelming. It was for Mary.

Many of Mary's fears were realized. Soon it became known that she was pregnant and there was talk in town about her and Joseph. There probably was speculation about her and someone else. Negative rumors fly so easily. The tongues of Nazareth wagged about Mary, some talking about what a disgrace she was to the community, some expressing self-righteousness covering private desires. Each day Mary's pregnancy became more obvious and the talk more incessant. What a fringe benefit this was to be blessed by God!

Then came the move to Bethlehem. It was a mixed blessing. Going to Bethlehem got Mary out of Nazareth and away from the stares, glares, and innuendos. However, moving to Bethlehem also took Mary away from family and the older women in the community who normally would have assisted her in the birth and early care of her child. To be blessed by God meant that Mary got to move seventy miles away to a community where she may not have known anyone and to give birth to her child in a stable.

The traumas of Mary's life did not end with the birth of her child. There was the decree that all male babies under two years of age be killed. Joseph packed up his family and headed for Egypt. They were becoming more like nomads than like a family settled in a home. Within a couple of years, they moved again. They started toward Bethlehem, but Joseph changed his mind and they went back to Nazareth, back to the poverty and the whispers. Eventually, the whispers subsided.

This is part of what it meant to Mary to be blessed of God. This discredits the idea that when you are doing God's will, loving God, and loving your fellow human beings as much as you love yourself, that all will be sweetness and light. Being a partner with God in the hazardous adventure of redemption is a complex issue. People's problems are too deep and too complex to be solved painlessly and neatly. To be blessed of God is to be invited to share in God's rescue operation. It involves hardship and complication, not unbroken ecstasy. Perhaps Mary knew something of what was involved in being blessed of God and that is why she responded initially with fear.

Mary became perplexed after her fear began to subside. Her perplexity was expressed in the question, "How can this be?" (Lk. 1:34 NRSV), referring to her pregnancy. Mary's trembling gave way to her timidity. To encounter God inviting you to join in a partnership in an adventure is to be overwhelmed. Either we see the task as so great and our resources and abilities so small that we can't make any difference, or we see so many obstacles facing us that must be overcome that we throw up our hands and exclaim it is impossible. Both of these approaches are present in Mary's question, "How can this be?" She is perplexed. But Gabriel had stayed around after he had said "Hello" and had a further statement to make. He told Mary that nothing was impossible for God. It is interesting, and perhaps more than coincidental, that more than thirty years later Jesus verbalized the same thing in his prayer, "Father, for you all things are possible" (Mk. 14:36 NRSV). I suspect that Mary learned through this experience that the grace of God was sufficient for her needs, and she communicated God's grace to her son as she nurtured and nourished him from infancy, through childhood, adolescence, and into adulthood.

Mary worked her way through this encounter with God's messenger and God's message. First, she was afraid, then she was perplexed, and then she became aware of God's grace at work. Once she sensed the grace of God giving her assurance and encouragement, Mary opened her life to God and told Gabriel, "Here I am, the servant of the Lord; let it be with me according to your word" (Lk. 1:38 NRSV). To be blessed of God just is not what we often think it is.

Mary's decision after working through all of these feelings was to respond in open trust. How many of us are willing to go to the length that Mary did in being blessed by God? With our middle-class value system, we measure our reputations above everything else. "What other people will think" is the altar where too many of us worship. Mary placed her life trustingly at God's disposal. God did not ask Mary to do miraculous things. God did ask Mary to be a partner in expressing God dwelling in human flesh. Mary's part in the process was her willingness and so is ours.

I recall reading somewhere a suggestion that compared this process to parliamentary procedure. God made a motion about how to become flesh and dwell among people and Mary said, "I second that motion." In every business session, motions require a second in order to be acted on, and this is the way God decided to run the universe. In a sense, God made a commitment to parliamentary procedure.

Probably all of us have been at a business session of some organization and witnessed motions that were made but died for lack of a second. This is at the bottom of many current problems. Why is there so much poverty, homelessness, prejudice, and ignorance? Why is there no song of love in the air? Why is the story of love not being told? Is it God's fault? Certainly not! God makes motions every day that the hungry be fed, the naked clothed, and the prisoners be redeemed, but what happens? We, unlike Mary, do not second God's motions. By our selfishness and lack of concern, God's good intentions die for lack of a second. A hungry child in a city slum prayed earnestly one Christmas for some food and toys, but nothing happened. She related this to a cynical friend who answered with a sneer: "What happened to this God of yours? Why did he not answer you?" To which the child responded simply: "Oh, I'm sure God heard me and told someone to bring me a Christmas gift, but I guess they just forgot." So often we fail God by failing to say by word and deed, "I second that motion."

To be blessed by God is to become a partner with God in the process of redemption and reconciliation. This involvement is hazardous, risky, and may be life-threatening. Mary's response was to be frightened, then to be timid, but then to experience the grace of God and to say with courage and trust to God, "I second your motion with my life." Look at what came of her faithfulness. The favor of God never assumes a life of ease. What emerged from this event was One who knew how to save people from their sins—One who also was willing to lay aside his reputation for the joy of reconciling people to God. Jesus learned firsthand from Mary how to live with the burden and the joy to be blessed of God, to be favored of God. Thus, she could tell the story of love with the words, "My soul magnifies the Lord" (Lk. 1:46).

May we learn to say as Mary did to God's motion of concern and care for people, "I second that motion." We are all invited to be blessed of God. If we know our history, our initial response will be one of fear because we would know that the biblical record clearly demonstrates that those favored of God have not fared well. Let us work through our fear to our timidity in the face of the perplexity of life and then discover that God's grace is sufficient for our needs. Then we will be able to respond to be favored of God by saying, "We belong to you, oh God, body and soul. Let it be to us—to me—according to your word." God makes a motion that the world be redeemed, that all people be reconciled to God. Let us second God's motion with our lives. What better way to tell the story of love! What better way to sing an old love song in a new way and a new day!

Joseph

We must build a bridge from the first Christmas to the present one in order for the drama of God coming to the world to have power and value in our lives. Exploring God's presence in the lives of the "star" characters in the drama can help us anticipate and experience God becoming flesh and dwelling in our lives.

Examining Joseph in this light has been especially helpful to me. Joseph has very much been a man in the background with regard to the Christmas narrative. He is not mentioned in Mark's Gospel, and he has only two references in John, both of which are references to Jesus as the son of Joseph. Luke mentions Joseph in concert with Mary. Only Matthew gives any elaboration about Joseph, and to call what Matthew writes an elaboration is an exaggeration.

Every nativity scene or Christmas play I have seen has Joseph in the background. Joseph is usually played in the Christmas plays by a nine-year-old boy wearing his dad's bathrobe and having a towel wrapped around his head. The boy is too shy to stand next to any girl, even if it is just for pretend. In these scenes, Joseph is at least two people removed from center stage. In the very center is someone's plastic doll representing Jesus and then there is Mary who is slightly behind the doll and just a step or two from center stage. Then comes Joseph somewhere in the background.

Very little biographical information is available about Joseph. His name means "may God add posterity." We choose names because we like the way they sound or because we want to name a person after someone that we like or to show that the infant is a continuation of a family. The Hebrew people chose a name because of what that name said about God. The name Joseph communicates that because God is the creator of life, God has made it possible to add posterity. The hope is that posterity will specifically be added to the one named Joseph. The Joseph of the Christmas story was a descendent of David who traced his family roots to Bethlehem. He worked as a carpenter, and either he or his family before him had migrated north from Judea and had settled in the hill town of Nazareth in Galilee. He met a girl in Nazareth to whom he became betrothed. To refer to Mary as a girl is not derogatory but does communicate her youthfulness.

Inferred through the story is that Joseph was older. Some have speculated that he was a widower with children. It was not uncommon for an older man with children to marry a young woman. In those days, marriage for a woman was the way that security and protection were guaranteed for her. The older a girl became before such an arrangement was made, the less likely an arrangement would be made. Most scholars assume that Joseph died early in Jesus' life, if not before he was grown, then certainly before Jesus began his ministry. The supporting evidence for this assumption is that Joseph is never mentioned after the time that he and Mary lost Jesus at the Temple when Jesus was twelve.

The specific setting for my focus on Joseph in this chapter is a personal crisis Joseph experienced and the series of events that surrounded it. To explore how people deal with crises in their lives and what their responses are in the midst of crises is quite revealing about the people, their security and stability, and will indicate whether we want people like them around us in the midst of difficult times in our lives.

Mary learned that she was pregnant, although she and Joseph were not married. Apparently, Mary told Joseph that she was expecting a child. The text does not say that Mary told Joseph, but it seems reasonable that she would have done so. Joseph was not clairvoyant, so he did not just guess that Mary was pregnant. Mary's pregnancy was devastating news for Joseph. Here was Joseph, having committed himself to spending the rest of his life with Mary, and before they had even said their wedding vows, she had betrayed him and destroyed his trust and confidence in her. I have seen betrayal and the breach of trust firsthand in people's lives, and I know the damage that it can do. Once the trust one person has in another is broken, there is nothing I know of that is more difficult to reestablish. To be betrayed goes to the core of a person's existence and to his or her opinion of himself or herself. There is nothing much worse that can happen to a sensitive person than to be betrayed and have trust broken. This is what happened to Joseph, and to observe Joseph's reactions is a revealing indicator of what Joseph was like. Such observation also discloses how Joseph was created in the image of God; it provides evidence of the kind of male role model that Jesus had as he was growing up.

Joseph's initial reaction to the news that Mary was pregnant was that his relationship with her was over. Joseph and Mary were betrothed to each other. To be betrothed was to be as close to being married as two people could be without being married. It was so close that some of the rules of marriage applied to people who were betrothed. For example, if the man died before they married, the woman was treated and related to as a widow. If the woman became involved with another man, she would be treated as an adulteress and by law could be stoned to death. When Joseph learned that Mary was pregnant, he considered the relationship to be over because Mary had broken her covenant, her commitment and promise to him.

Joseph is described as a man who did what was right. This refers to his piety and righteousness. Joseph could not consider continuing a relationship with an adulteress because that was wrong according to the religious laws of the day. This understanding of religious purity and cleanliness was based on the old adage of guilt by association. Many still operate and relate on this premise. Often our attitudes and actions convey that we believe bad will have more influence than good. In this sense, we tend to believe more in evil than we do in God. Joseph wanted to do what was right in the situation with Mary.

But there was another characteristic of Joseph that created a conflict for him. He was a sensitive, compassionate human being. He was caught in the bind of not wanting to associate with one who had done wrong and yet being sensitive to the pain, hurt, and need of the one who had done wrong. He did not want to embarrass or disgrace Mary publicly. But why should he not? She had betrayed him, and soon her presence in public would disgrace him. Joseph had every right to disgrace her. This time the law was on his side. Joseph was justified to "let Mary have it." But Joseph's hurt feelings and legal considerations could not overrule something else in Joseph's personality: his compassion for this woman who was down. Joseph just was not constituted emotionally to step on Mary when she was down.

Joseph was neither apathetic nor vindictive. He did not say, "Oh, it doesn't matter; just forget it." This approach would only have cheapened the relationship. Joseph was serious about his divorce plans, but he was sensitive that another human being was involved. He did not explode in vindictiveness nor write Mary off as hopeless and worthless. Joseph took a merciful, compassionate approach toward this tragic and devastating crisis in his life. It may be here more than anywhere else that Joseph revealed that he was made in the image of God. With every justification lined up on his side to destroy Mary, he permitted his compassion and care for another human being to overrule his anger, hurt, and resentment. He resisted both the letter and the spirit of the law. He considered Mary's situation and needs in deciding that he would quietly and privately dissolve his relationship with her.

A second characteristic about Joseph that is revealed through his personal crisis is his openness to mystery, wonder, and possibilities. Mary added another load of jolting news just as Joseph was recovering from the shock wave that Mary was pregnant. She said that the baby was conceived by God. This had to be either the most creative or the craziest suggestion as the source of pregnancy that anybody ever devised. God gets credit and blame for a lot of things in life, but this was a new one as far as Joseph was concerned. Only a fool would believe such a story! You would think Joseph would just go off stage laughing and leave Mary in her own world. This was a double-barreled shock. Such a claim that God was in all of this was more than a person's mind could handle, but according to Matthew, Joseph considered this. He turned it over in his mind rather than dismissing it at once as foolishness. This is amazing. If a woman entered a hospital today to give birth to a child and claimed that the baby was conceived by God, who would believe her? But Joseph took such an incredible claim by Mary and considered it.

Then Joseph had a dream. Dreams are evidence that people's minds are at work all the time. Dreams are attempts by the subconscious to deal with issues and situations that have not yet been resolved. One of the major causes of dreams is fear. So it was for Joseph. He had learned that Mary was pregnant and he was afraid. The messenger who appeared in his dream told him, "Don't be afraid." I suspect Joseph responded, "That's easy for you to say. You're not the one having to live through all of this, facing family and friends and neighborhood gossips. What do you mean, 'Don't be afraid'?" Every person who ever stepped up to an altar to commit himself or herself in marriage has been afraid. The tension and fear are even greater when other issues cloud the marriage issue.

Joseph was willing to consider possibilities as a result of his dream. He did not conclude, "Because I can't conceive of it, it is impossible." He did not throw around the word *impossible* in arrogance, nor did he "sit in the seat of the scornful." Joseph was open to the possibility and willing to let God be God and not restrict God to narrow limitations. This is the nature of faith. Plenty of people have already decided what is possible and what is not. They refuse to look beyond those self-imposed limits. We can speak with some certainty about what has happened, but there is no absolute authority on what will happen.

Joseph related positively to the mystery of life. Later, when the wise men came for a visit and related their conversation with Herod to Joseph and Mary, it stirred concern in Joseph. Once again he dreamed and this time he dreamed of safety for his family in Egypt. Something in the wise men's words triggered fear in Joseph and he dreamed as a result. Later, in his longing to return to his homeland, Joseph dreamed again and followed the intuition of his dream; however, when he learned that Archelaus was ruler in Judea, Joseph decided that Galilee would be a better place to settle, set up shop, and raise a family. Joseph was open to possibilities in life.

A third characteristic worth noting in Joseph is that he was willing to venture out in life on the basis of his hunches and impressions. Courage is required to take the kind of action that Joseph took based on Mary's word and a dream he had had. But Joseph was willing to take the risk. There were several adjustments necessary once Joseph had made the commitment. First, he decided they needed to get out of Nazareth, and rightly so. Who was going to believe their story? After all, Joseph had difficulty believing it, and if he began talking about dreams and angels, the people would laugh them out of town! So why not just leave quietly? Joseph decided they would take the initiative and go on their own. They went to Bethlehem and no explanation was necessary there. Have you taken similar action in your life, like moving to a new community or changing schools or changing jobs? Have you explained your relief by saying that you don't have to explain anything to anybody? Joseph was a man of decisiveness and sensitivity who trusted nuances of guidance that more cautious people would have avoided.

And the Word became flesh and dwelt in Joseph. Look what God did. God entrusted the growth and development of Jesus to Joseph. Examining Joseph's life is revealing of the characteristics of God that are evident in Joseph: compassion, acceptance, grace, openness to possibilities, and a willingness to venture. God has been venturing from the time the creation began. God has been taking risks ever since. God took a risk with Joseph.

Jesus grew up in this climate, relating to this man Joseph. Jesus discovered and experienced compassion, mercy, and tenderness to be excellent human qualities of men and women. Is it so surprising that later in his life, after Joseph had passed and Jesus was fully into his ministry, that a woman who was guilty of adultery was brought to him for a judgment, one whom Jesus would have been justified in making a public example of by having her stoned, said, "I don't condemn you. Go and sin no more"?

Years later, when life was closing in on Jesus and he found himself cornered in the Garden of Gethsemane, he prayed, "With you all things are possible," because he had grown up in a home and related to a father who was open to the mystery of life and who refused to close the door on options, alternatives, and possibilities.

Joseph may have been a man in the background for centuries, but that does not mean we should overlook his life, the impact his life had on Jesus, or the revelation that his life offers us. We can learn from Joseph what it means to be created in the image of God. And God became flesh and dwelt in Joseph.

Jesus

One of the first tasks that parents of newborn infants have is to name the child. In our culture, the hospital staff gets nervous if parents don't have a name for the baby by the second day. Parents had better not even think of leaving the hospital with their baby unnamed. What if parents told the staff they were not going to name their child until eight days later? Panic!

Well, this is exactly what Joseph and Mary did. Of course, there was no attending obstetrician or nurse standing around the stable telling them they couldn't leave until they gave that boy a name. Besides, it was part of their religious custom to have a son circumcised and give him his name on the eighth day. Normally, circumcision and naming of a child occurred in the home because the mother was considered ceremonially unclean and could not participate in any activities at the place of worship. Some of the religious rules recorded in Leviticus jolt us today and raise questions about their meaning and purpose, like the evidence that the ancient Jews had a widespread preference for sons and regarded girls as inferior.

Childbirth has always been filled with mystery and wonder. Even though we know and understand so much about pregnancy and birth today, are able to know the sexual identification of an infant before it is born, and can determine its approximate weight, childbirth still contains mystery and wonder. The mystery and wonder are the result of the arrival of new life while there is great risk to the mother and the infant at the time of the birth. In the ancient world, and in many parts of the world today, the infant mortality rate is extremely high. The ancients realized that the mother and child should be properly protected. The ceremony of circumcision and naming were partly for the protection of the mother and child.

The naming of the child also was a means of giving thanks to God for the gift of life. Joseph and Mary wanted to link Jesus' life with all the rich inheritance of Israel. Originally, every religious rite and ceremony was an effort to express a spiritual purpose. As long as rites and ceremonies have purpose, there is value in honoring them. It became custom early in Christendom to baptize infants, and even today, most of Christendom baptizes infants. This is a very good thing. There is no confusion about who gets the credit. The baby will not remember what went on. No one attempts to discuss what the experience meant to the infant. But it is a dramatic way of saying that salvation is something God does.

There are at least two temptations in the tradition of believer's baptism. One is for those being baptized to conclude that they are in the water in response to a choice they were wise enough to make. The other temptation is for people to secretly entertain the notion that if their witness had not been so effective, the person might not be standing there, waist deep in water. We can easily forget that faith is a gift, and it comes from God.

When it came to that significant moment of giving their infant a name, Joseph and Mary chose a name that carried meaning. Most names have meanings that have been derived from people who have had those names and given meaning to them. Often names are words chosen from one language and transliterated into another to convey an idea or express an attitude. The prophet Hosea gave his children some horrible names (Not Pitied and Not My People, for example) to make a point. The name "Jesus" conveyed meaning. It comes from the Hebrew "Joshua" that comes from a more ancient word "Yehoshua" that means "Yahweh is salvation." Jesus was a very popular name in the first century, just as popular names today run in cycles. Josephus, a Jewish historian, found at least nineteen people in the first century who were named Jesus. Jesus Barrabbas is an example in the New Testament. The popularity of the name may reflect the rising tide of expectation of salvation and deliverance among the Jews following the Maccabean revolt.

To distinguish the Jesus we are most familiar with from others, the New Testament writers refer to him as Jesus of Nazareth, Jesus, Son of David, the Galilean, the Nazarene, or The Prophet. The Greek-speaking Gentile church preferred titles with theological connotations, so as Christianity spread and included more and more Gentiles, Christ, which means "messiah" or "anointed one," became a popular name. Jesus became identified as Christ Jesus or Jesus Christ.

Not long after Jesus was named, his parents took him to the Temple for the first time. He was forty days old. Apparently, the two ceremonies of purification and the redemption of the firstborn had been united by this time in Judaism. The Jews placed great emphasis on the blood of a person or an animal. Life resided in the blood for the Jews. From that emphasis has come the identification that something is the lifeblood of an organization. Of course, the blood supply is essential as the transportation system for nutriments, oxygen, carbon dioxide, and disease fighters. A person is seriously ill who has a blood disease or disorder, regardless of what it is.

The loss of blood in Judaism was considered a loss of life. The mystery of life was related to blood because blood was lost during childbirth. Usually, the loss of blood accompanied the death of an animal and often accompanied the death of a person. Because of this, a woman was considered unclean for forty days after the birth of a son, and eighty days after the birth of a daughter. She was to offer a lamb and a pigeon, or two pigeons if she could not afford a lamb, when she went to the Temple for the rite of purification. These offerings served as tangible expressions of the awareness that in childbirth the life-giving forces and the life-taking forces are especially present. These gifts were expressions of thanksgiving for the gift of life.

The rite of the redemption of the firstborn was a religious ceremony acknowledging that the firstborn and, in essence, all things belonged to God. The offering given was to acknowledge this and, in a sense, to ask God's permission to have the firstborn.

Luke tells us about the three ceremonies—circumcision, purification, and redemption of the firstborn—in which the infant Jesus participated. All three were ways for his parents to acknowledge and act out their convictions that a child is a gift from God.

The Stoics believed that a child was loaned to parents by God. Kahlil Gibran has expressed a similar idea in *The Prophet*:

And a woman who held a babe against her bosom said, Speak to us of Children.
And he said:
Your children are not your children. They are the sons and daughters of
    Life's longing for itself.
They come through you but not from you, And though they are with you yet
    they belong not to you.
You may give them your love but not your thoughts,
For they have their own thoughts.
You may house their bodies but not their souls,
For their souls dwell in the house of tomorrow, which you cannot visit, not
    even in your dreams.
You may strive to be like them, but seek not to make them like you.
For life goes not backward nor tarries with yesterday.
You are the bows from which your children as living arrows are sent forth.
The archer sees the mark upon the path of the infinite, and He bends you
    with his might that His arrows may go swift and far.
Let your bending in the Archer's hand be for gladness;
For even as He loves the arrow that flies, so He loves also the bow that is stable.[3]

Luke went to great effort in his account of Jesus' life to communicate with his readers that Jesus was very much like other people. He was born into a poor family, but a family devout in its commitment and worship of God. Luke tells us that Jesus was born, circumcised, given a name, participated in the rites of purification and the firstborn as did all Jewish male babies, and that he grew up like other boys in his time.

Luke combined the celebration of the gift of life coming in the form of an infant and the gratitude that his parents expressed for this gift through the rites and ceremonies of their covenant community. All of this and much more is wrapped up in the name and person of Jesus whose name means "God is salvation" or "God is deliverer." Luke wrote that this extraordinary deliverer, emancipator, son of God, had an ordinary, common beginning. When Mrs. Martin Luther King Sr. died several years ago, Andrew Young remarked concerning the dates on her tombstone (1904–1974): "She didn't have much to do with those two dates. But she had a lot to do with the dash!" Great people are born like all other people. However, great people seem to develop openness to the needs of people and openness to the presence and direction of God. Jesus had little to do with his birth or his death but he had a lot to do with what went on in between them. To call his name is to acknowledge that both life and salvation are gifts—gifts from God to any and to all who receive them.

The Supporting Cast

In analyzing my storytelling ability, my wife has suggested that I tend to give mainly the "nuts and bolts" of the story, but often leave out the exciting sidelights and subplots. This seems also to have been the approach of those who recorded the drama of God coming to the world. I have already indicated how little information is available about the lead characters. This is even more the case with the supporting cast. The supporting cast members in this drama are Elizabeth, Herod, the innkeeper, Simeon, and the Magi.

Elizabeth

Elizabeth is so obscure that *Nave's Topical Bible* gives only two bits of information about her. She was the wife of Zechariah and the mother of John the Baptist. *The Interpreter's Dictionary of the Bible* briefly expands on this information. Only Luke gives any ink to Elizabeth's role. Even his comments are brief and serve mainly to introduce John the Baptist into the story. For me to focus so much attention on Elizabeth may support the adage that "fools rush in where angels dare to tread."

The name Elizabeth means "God is an oath," or "God is good fortune." There are two Elizabeths mentioned in scripture. The other one was the wife of Aaron, and they were the first priestly family of Israel. Some circumstantial evidence suggests that the Elizabeth in Luke's Gospel was from a priestly family. Zechariah was a priest from a priestly family. In a sense, Elizabeth's marriage to Zechariah would have been considered ideal; however, there was one hitch in the idealism of this union: Elizabeth had not given birth to a child. Elizabeth must have questioned the meaning of her name, "God is good fortune." Childlessness was interpreted as punishment for sin in the Middle East, especially for the Israelites. A woman's worth was measured by her ability to give birth to a child and her worth was greatly enhanced if she gave birth to a son.

The birth of a child, especially a son, was an occasion of great joy and celebration. Friends and local musicians gathered near the house when the time of birth was near. When the birth was announced, if the baby was a boy, the musicians broke into music and song and there was universal congratulations and rejoicing. If the child was a girl, the musicians went away silently and regretfully. Although few people today interpret childlessness as the result of sin, many do believe there is something "wrong" with a married woman who has no children. Many never give any thought to the possibility that there may be something genetically related to a couple not having children. For some people, it is inconceivable that a woman would choose not to conceive.

Elizabeth felt the judgment and condemnation of her community. She had been married several years and had no children. The community concluded there was something wrong with her. Who knows how many "friends" she had who had encouraged her to repent of her sins so she could give birth to a child! When the news leaked that Elizabeth was pregnant, there were those who said, "Well, well, the old gal finally confessed. I wonder what sin she had committed."

Luke uses Elizabeth's pregnancy to connect her to Mary, the mother of Jesus. The messenger greets Mary with the double news of her pregnancy and Elizabeth's. The interpretation given is that Elizabeth's pregnancy is evidence of God's power. "Remember your relative Elizabeth. It is said that she cannot have children, but she herself is now six months pregnant, even though she is very old. For there is nothing God cannot do" (Lk. 1:36–37 TEV).

How old did a woman have to be to be *very* old? There is no way to determine that. Some guesstimates have Mary being between thirteen and sixteen. In this context, a woman who was twenty-five who had been married ten years or more, which was common, would have been an old woman. We do not know how closely related Elizabeth and Mary were. The only information is Luke's identification of Elizabeth as Mary's kinswoman. They probably were cousins, but whether first or fourth is anyone's guess.

Mary hurried off to visit Elizabeth soon after receiving the double pregnancy news. Apparently, the purpose for Mary's visit was to verify Elizabeth's pregnancy. If Elizabeth were pregnant, then maybe what was happening to Mary would be a little more believable, at least to Mary if to no one else.

Mary took one look at Elizabeth and knew she was pregnant, but then she stayed for three months. Why? Why didn't Mary go visit her parents, if she was going to visit anyone? Where is Joseph during this three-month period? How was he feeling? What questions were rambling through his mind?

Let's speculate on some reasons why Mary visited Elizabeth and stayed three months. Since Elizabeth also was pregnant, she was someone Mary sensed would understand and empathize with her. They had pregnancy in common.

It happens today. Two women, total strangers to each other, meet. Both are pregnant. A conversation develops as they share details about their pregnancies, their due dates, their health, their expectations. "Is this your first child?" "Have you had any problems?" Quickly, they begin to know each other. Or a casual friendship becomes a close-knit relationship between two expectant mothers.

Mary and Elizabeth shared being pregnant at the same time as well as it being the first pregnancy for each. Joy and support came from this common first experience as each identified with the feelings of the other. Bonding occurred as they shared and compared fears and feelings.

Perhaps Mary also went to visit Elizabeth because Elizabeth was older and had been married for several years. Mary perceived Elizabeth to be secure and settled, and she hoped to draw strength from Elizabeth.

Elizabeth and Mary also shared the hurt of gossip. Mary knew what some of the comments would be when word got out that she was pregnant and unmarried. She had heard those biting, judgmental, unmerciful words spoken about others. She did not expect she would be an exception. She knew what her standing in the community would be. Maybe that's why she did not go to visit her mother. Parents often are so concerned about their reputations that they hang signs around their children's necks that read: "What will people think of me when they see you?"

Mary knew Elizabeth would understand because she had experienced the prejudice and hurtful barbs of people for several years. Elizabeth knew how sharp and painful tongues could be, and she had weathered that storm for a long time. Mary anticipated Elizabeth would understand and maybe having one person understand her would provide the strength Mary needed for the journey that was ahead of her.

Why did Mary stay for three months? I could understand a week or two, but three months? How did Zechariah and Elizabeth feel having a relative plop down on their doorstep and become a permanent fixture? Whatever Zechariah felt, he couldn't say anything because Elizabeth's pregnancy had knocked him speechless.

Some issues and situations in life require time and distance in order for people to adjust healthily. Mary needed both time and distance to deal with all that was happening in her life. And she went to one whom she anticipated would empathize and understand her. I think she found a true soul mate there. That is why she stayed three months. It took her that long to sort things out and get herself together emotionally to have the strength and stamina to face the wagging tongues of Nazareth. Indeed, Elizabeth provided the support she needed and was a vital part of the supporting cast of the drama of God coming to the world.

Mary's visit with Elizabeth raises many other questions. Why did Mary leave just before John was born? Did Elizabeth and Mary drift apart after their pregnancies? Did they visit each other again? How often? What influence did each have on the other's child? Did they compare notes on their sons? How were John and Jesus alike and different as infants, toddlers, children, and young men? Did Elizabeth and Mary ever talk about the revolutionary ways that their sons went about their worship and service of God? Were Elizabeth and Mary supportive of each other during other crises? When John was beheaded, was Mary supportive of Elizabeth? When Jesus was crucified, was Elizabeth there for Mary again?

Elizabeth demonstrates for us what a supportive person can do. Everybody needs somebody who understands, who sees and feels life from her perspective. Certainly, Elizabeth was that for Mary. I nominate her for her best supporting role to Mary in the drama of dramas, the drama of God coming to the world.

Herod

Supporting characters are not always the people with whom we identify or like, but their roles are essential in developing the drama and enabling the story to be told. Herod played an essential part in the drama of God coming to the world, but certainly not because God wanted him to play the role he played. Actually, Herod was the villain in this drama because of his action and treatment of others.

Several Herods are named in the Bible, but the one in this drama is known as Herod the Great. He was the son of the Idumean Antipater. He was half Jew and half Idumean and was given the title "King of Judea" around 40 B.C.E. by the Roman senate with the support of Anthony and Octavius. Herod was useful to the Romans in wars, especially the civil wars in Palestine. He was the only ruler of Palestine who had any success at keeping order. He was a great builder, having rebuilt the Temple in Jerusalem, built a theater in Jerusalem, and an amphitheater nearby. He also built a royal palace and rebuilt several fortresses. Herod had ten wives and fifteen children.

Herod could be a generous person. He remitted taxes in times of difficulty, and he actually melted his own gold plate to buy corn for starving people during the famine of 25 B.C.E. And yet, Herod was indifferent and unconcerned about Jewish ethics or fidelity to Jewish law or standards.

A flaw in Herod's character appeared early in his reign and seemed only to worsen with age. He was suspicious of people, at times insanely suspicious. Anyone whom he slightly suspected, even if only in his own mind, as a rival to his power was promptly eliminated. Herod could be a cruel man and often was. He had his favorite wife executed, a strange way to treat a favorite, executed his brother-in-law who was the high priest, and executed several of his sons and others who were close to him biologically and emotionally. He lived in fear of intrigue or assassination and especially did not trust the Maccabean family into which he had married.

Herod was greatly upset when the Magi came to Bethlehem and asked to see the one *born* king of the Jews. He was king by intrigue, maneuver, Roman appointment, and the constant use of the sword and execution to eliminate Maccabean rivals. Herod was an insecure, frightened man. Nothing he ever did or accomplished calmed his fear—not building, not commanding an army, not dominating and controlling people, not even eliminating those that he imagined might oppose him. Herod became so frightened, so suspicious, that he imagined his own death would cause joy in the land. (This may have been his one well-founded fear.) He gave the order that at his death, the oldest child in each home was to be put to death in an effort to make the nation weep.

When Herod learned from the Magi about one born king, he instructed them that when they had found this king to report the location of this king to him. The Magi did not report back to Herod, and he was furious. He took his anger out on innocent infants. He had all male children in Bethlehem two years of age and younger killed. Herod delivered the mail of his fury and fear to the wrong address, but he was trying to make certain that whoever this born king was would be eliminated. The number slain was of no consequence to Herod as long as he thought that he got his intended victim. Although Bethlehem was not a large town, Herod's decree meant the slaughter of twenty to thirty children who had done nothing wrong other than having been born at the wrong time from Herod's fearful perspective.

Herod was a frightened man. Rather than dealing with his fears, Herod's fears dealt with him and controlled him. Herod was king—king of Judea and king of fear.

Herod's life illustrates clearly that fear is real even when the danger is only imagined. Psychiatrist W. Hugh Missildine has pointed out that fear is one of the earliest emotions an infant experiences. He indicates that fears tend to group themselves into three categories: the fear of falling, the fear of loud noises or catastrophes, and the fear of being abandoned.[4] These fears affect people throughout their lives. The fear of falling gets translated in adult life into the fear of failing—the fear of losing a job or esteem or one's place in life. The fear of loud noises becomes the fear of death, death of spouse or children, the fear of war or nuclear holocaust, the fear of economic collapse or the destruction of reputation. There also is the recurring fear of abandonment. What if my ideas dried up while I'm writing this book? What if my friends decided to have nothing to do with me because of my position on an issue?

My work with people in dealing with their personal crises has revealed how often people are motivated by fear. Children are not honest with their parents because they are "afraid" of how their parents will respond. A person refuses a church leadership position because she is "afraid" she will not meet the congregation's expectations. A spouse needs to tell his companion about the distance he senses in their relationship, but he is "afraid" of her reaction.

Fear often is enlarged and expanded by stereotyping people. Hitler feared he was inferior to the Jews. He exterminated millions of them, claiming he and his kind were a superior race. The proliferation of nuclear weapons is the result of fear. Lip service is paid to health care and education, but our fear motivates us to abandon the "unemployable"—the elderly, the young, and the poor in the name of national security.

Herod was king of fear and now fear has come to rule in our lives. With fear running rampant, people panic and terrorism becomes the order of the day. Fear piled on fear leads to catastrophe. There is a need for personal and national patience. More than one person has observed that in trying to be the richest person in the world, there will always be a Bill Gates ahead of you. However, having five minutes more patience than your opposition will win every time.

Fear got the best of Herod and destroyed him. Our fears are getting the best of us. They will destroy us if we allow them to rule our lives. Catholic monk Thomas Merton often exhorted peacemakers during the Vietnam War era: "We have to have a deep, patient compassion for the fears of men, for the fears and irrational mania of those who hate and condemn us."[5] Herod and those who have followed in his footsteps clearly demonstrate that we do have much to fear from fear itself. Fear is real even when the danger is only imagined.

Fear feeds on mistrust and then feeds mistrust. Thus, a vicious cycle of mistrust develops, fear escalates, and we become frozen in fear. Herod is one of the best examples of a destructive response to life. Herod's suspicions and fears were unfounded, but he became so frightened that his fears controlled him. All he seemed capable of doing was destroying everyone around him. He was the King of Fear. To see him, to examine his approach to life can help us to see more clearly that love casts out fear. It is time for us to switch loyalties. For too long we have followed the king of fear, fed our fears, and turned over control of our lives to fear. The drama of God coming to the world is to act out for us that love casts out fear. This drama calls for us to switch loyalties, to cease following the king of fear and to begin following the prince of peace.

The Innkeeper

The drama is becoming increasingly complicated. One of the key supportive roles in every Christmas pageant I have ever seen has been the innkeeper. Always a boy in an oversized bathrobe mustering up his gruffest voice tells Joseph that his Best Eastern Motel is full. There is no room for Joseph and Mary, regardless of their circumstances. Did they not know all their relatives would be streaming into Bethlehem to fill out their census cards? Why did they wait so late to travel? Why did they not send ahead for reservations? They knew they were coming and they knew what their circumstances were. Why should the innkeeper look out for them?

Although the innkeeper has provided a valuable dimension to Christmas pageants through the centuries, there is a technical problem. No innkeeper is mentioned in the original script, that being the biblical narratives of the drama of God coming to the world. However, for the sake of tradition and the wording in the script that says, "and there was no room for them in the inn," let's assume that there was an innkeeper. After all, inns do not keep themselves and we can safely conclude that there was an innkeeper for what has become the best-known no-name inn in the world.

Traditionally, the innkeeper has been viewed as a callous villain who cared nothing for the needs of people, especially people in a crisis. He (given the historical context it is safe to assume that the innkeeper was a man) also has been portrayed as more interested in making money than doing anything to assist people in need. This is the result of projection by people in retelling the story because there is no indication that finances had anything to do with the no vacancy. The inn was crowded, and there was no room for two peasants who any minute were going to become three.

Examination of the phrase "no room" has disclosed that the basic meaning of this phrase is "there was no appropriate place for them in the inn." The inns in the first century certainly were nothing like our motels. They were little more than a courtyard off which stalls opened. What people got for their money was a place to hitch their animal, some straw to lie down on, and a wall that would break the wind at night. There certainly was no privacy. Such an arrangement was not an appropriate place to give birth to a child.

But what were Joseph and Mary doing waiting until the last minute to get a place to stay? Maybe they hadn't waited until the last minute. Professor William Hull has pointed out the possibility that Joseph and Mary took up residence in one of the local inns in Bethlehem and lived there for several months prior to Jesus' birth.[6] Joseph worked at his carpenter's trade to provide for them. Supporting this interpretation are the facts that Joseph could have gone to Bethlehem for the census and left Mary in Nazareth. It also does not make sense that he would wait until Mary was in her ninth month of pregnancy before he would begin the eighty mile journey from Nazareth to Bethlehem.

No doubt there was a time frame in which the census was to be completed, but surely it covered more than the last couple of weeks of Mary's pregnancy.

All of this causes me to look at the innkeeper from a new perspective. Joseph and Mary have been in Bethlehem for some time, and obviously, Mary is near the date for the birth of her child. The innkeeper could tell that this couple was approaching an awkward moment. Here was a young woman separated from some of the older women she knew who could have been counted on to help with the birth. She also was living in an open courtyard, hardly an appropriate place for childbirth.

What is the likelihood that the innkeeper took it upon himself to find a place of privacy for Mary and Joseph? What the innkeeper came up with was a stable; actually, it probably was a cave. It may have been the kind of place where shepherds kept their sheep part of the year. Later in the script, Luke says that it was the season when the shepherds were spending nights in the fields with their flocks. They weren't using the stable space. Here was a secluded place that would be more appropriate than an open courtyard to give birth to a child and have some privacy.

Maybe the innkeeper was more of a gentleman and less of a villain than we have given him credit for. The innkeeper was probably busier than usual if Bethlehem was crowded with visitors in town to register for the census, but he was not so busy that he would not take time to do what he could to help two strangers who were in a difficult crisis. We prefer to make the innkeeper a villain. We can project our hostility and frustration on him and deny that we are anything like that. But if we start considering him as a person of compassion who did what he could to help two strangers, then that calls for us to use our resources to meet the needs of strangers who come into our lives. Maybe we do not want the drama of God coming to the world getting that dramatic, that close and personal.

To make this part of the script even more dramatic, just a couple of years ago I came across another perspective. Kenneth E. Bailey is a Middle Eastern expert who resides at the Ecumenical Center for Biblical Studies in Tantur, a few miles outside modern Bethlehem. Bailey reinterprets the narrative of Jesus' birth from the perspective of one who has spent most of his life in the Middle East.

He notes that in the narrative that says there was "no place for them in the inn" (Lk. 2:7 RSV), the Greek word for "inn" is actually *kataluma*, which means "guest room" and does not imply an inn as the forerunner to our hotels and motels. Later, in the story of the Good Samaritan, the Samaritan takes the wounded man to a *pandokheion*, which does mean "inn," the forerunner to hotel. If Luke had meant to say "inn" in the narrative of Jesus' birth, he would have used *pandokheion*, not *kataluma*.[7]

Bailey observed that Westerners need to understand the arrangement of a typical Middle Eastern house. In such a house, the living room often doubles as a guest room. If there are overnight visitors, they sleep in this room. Adjacent to this room, but at a slightly lower level—as in a split-level house—is a rough, outer room into which the family's animals are usually brought at night, especially during colder weather. They are led away in the morning and the room is swept. The manger for the animals is another feature of the Middle Eastern home. It is built into the floor of the upper level, or living room level. The animals can reach the manger but cannot walk in it.

A Middle Easterner reading the Gospel story would immediately recognize its events this way.[8] Joseph and Mary came to Bethlehem, where they were among numerous relatives. We are told that Mary had just visited her cousin Elizabeth, the mother of John the Baptist, and Joseph, who was "of the house and lineage of David," would have had many kinsfolk in the region, since it was his hometown. They, like Joseph, had to go to Bethlehem to register for the census.

It would have been unthinkable for them to stay in a public inn. Instead, they sought out the home of relatives. In addition, the hospitality customs of the Middle East call for people to welcome sojourners and strangers. Certainly, kinfolk would be welcome. There were other relatives in Bethlehem as well, so that there was no room in the *kataluma*, guest room, and they had to sleep in the lower, outer room, the one into which animals were often brought at night. When Jesus was born, he was wrapped in swaddling clothes, (a Middle Eastern tradition) and laid in the manger, where all the folks in the living room could admire him, too.[9]

Thus, Jesus was not born into the cold, forbidding atmosphere usually depicted by our Western understanding of the text, but among extended family members gathered in Bethlehem for the same reason Joseph was there. The Savior of the world was born in the midst of a loving, doting family, among aunts and uncles and cousins known by his parents and loved by them.

Being home for Christmas is a compelling desire of many people. In one sense, Jesus himself was home for Christmas. He was born in a real home, in the bosom of a large family. This was real incarnation, to be born as other Middle Eastern children were born and often are born to this day.

Why does it matter anyway? Why do we always associate Christmas with home? I suppose it has to do with tradition, with a sense of belonging and happiness we have all experienced at Christmastime. Many of our best memories are built around being home at Christmas. We remember the beauty of childhood Christmas trees, decked in lights and covered with icicles—the magical packages under the tree—the smell of bread baking—music from a favorite recording—the sense of secrecy and excitement as the great day drew near—the wonderful feeling of love and sharing, when even the most irritable and gruff members of the family seemed to grow soft and tender. Christmas and home seem naturally to go together.

But there is something more than this. It has to do with a deeper sense of home that we feel at Christmastime—a sense of cosmic belonging—as if, at this special time of the year, we come closer to eternity than at any other time. Perhaps it is with the drama of an inn, a Middle Eastern home, that the veil between this life and some other plane of existence seems thinnest, almost as if we could simply step from one side to the other. Bethlehem is the doorway, and we sometimes imagine we can hear the angel choirs a little beyond.

The German poet Holderin, one of the contemporary existentialists, has written of the essential "homelessness" of all of us—our inability ever to feel completely at home in this world. There is always a longing, a yearning for something more, for something beyond, for a life we can suspect but cannot touch.

It is this homelessness that haunts the works of our greatest writers, musicians, and artists. They know that humanity is not the measure of everything, that there is a mystery beyond us, impinging on our lives but never satisfying us in this life. It lures us, draws us, teases and torments us, until at last we give up the ghost and embrace it fully. Perhaps this is why we have harassed the innkeeper for so long, made him into a villain, made him a larger-than-life figure, and written him into the script even when he was not there.

The Christmas story is the drama of God contacting us from beyond, of our having heard from home. This is what the excitement was all about— what it is still about. In Bethlehem, whether through an innkeeper or in a typical Middle Eastern home of relatives, Joseph and Mary sensed God had gotten in touch with them, assured them of life in some other plane of existence, and heard God say, "Here is my gift of love. There is room for you. You have a home with me."[10]

What my thinking about the innkeeper has caused me to do is to have a new way of looking at old things. The drama of God coming to the world through an innkeeper or Joseph's relatives in Bethlehem has challenged me to be sensitive to people around me as the innkeeper or Joseph's Bethlehem relatives may have been. The drama of God coming to the world always seems to result in matching people's needs with resources to meet those needs. Is there any more exhilarating meaning and mystery and drama than this?

Simeon

Only the innkeeper is more obscure than Simeon in God's drama, and only Luke has anything to say about Simeon. Simeon is portrayed as a righteous and devout man who lived in Jerusalem at the time of Jesus' birth.

The Jews of the biblical centuries believed that they would some day be masters of the world and lords of nations, but there was no consensus on how this would occur. Some believed that a great champion would descend on them. Some were convinced that another king from David's family would rise and all the old glories would be revived. There were those who believed God would intervene in the world through supernatural means. And there were those who were convinced that by military might God's reign would be enforced in the world.

In contrast to all of these views were a few people in Palestine known as the Quiet in the Land. These people had no dreams of violence, or power, or armies; they believed in a life of prayer and quiet watchfulness until God would come. Simeon was like these people, if not one of them. He was waiting for the day for God to comfort the people.

Simeon was confident this would happen. The question for Simeon was *when* God would comfort the people. Simeon lived on the premise that he would see the Anointed One of God. The word "Christ" is a translation of the word "messiah," which means "anointed one." The "Anointed One" was the one appointed by God to deliver people from bondage and free people to worship and serve God. The premise of Simeon's living was established on the promise he claimed he had from God that he would not die before he had seen the Anointed One. No one knows how Simeon received this promise. Evidence is plentiful that God communicated to Simeon just like God communicates to you and me. How are you certain God has made a promise to you? That's the kind of certainty Simeon had!

The sun was setting on Simeon's life, but not on his confidence. He was at the Temple when the moment finally came. When he saw Mary and Joseph, Simeon rushed over and took one look at the baby through his cataracts and asked if he could hold him. Simeon had grabbed Jesus up in his arms before either of them could respond. Simeon's confidence gave way to celebration with tenderness, joy, and excitement as he spoke a blessing for this tiny newborn. What Luke says he said became a hymn of the church known as "*Nunc Dimittis.*"

> Now, Lord, you have kept your promise,
>   And you may let your servant go in peace.
> With my own eyes I have seen your salvation,
>   Which you have prepared in the presence of all peoples:
> A light to reveal your will to the Gentiles
>   And bring glory to your people Israel. (Lk. 2:29–32 TEV)

Simeon's blessing had personal meaning and universal application. Simeon desired one thing before he died: to see the unfolding of God's promise. A personality was needed for this to happen. He would die content if, just once, he could look on the face that had the light of God in it. He saw hope for his people when he held Jesus in his arms. He knew that God's salvation and deliverance, the journey through bondage into freedom, would be expressed by and through a human being. All of the hope and confidence Simeon had held for years, he now projected onto this tiny infant. Simeon, who had lived his hope in God, believed that in the new generation represented by the baby he held in his arms, the hope to which he had clung would become a reality for all people. Simeon said now he was ready to go in peace, to die. Simeon is one of those fortunate people who comes to the end of life with the conviction that life could not have been more rewarding and meaningful.

While there is great personal meaning in Simeon's blessing, the universal application must not be obscured or forgotten. We prefer to be sentimental over the birth of Jesus and leave the story there. We want to end the story with, "The shepherds went back, singing praises to God for all they had heard and seen; it had been just as the angel had told them" (Lk.. 2:20 TEV).

The last words of Simeon's blessing must not be lost or forgotten: "A light to reveal your will to the Gentiles and bring glory to your people, Israel" (Lk. 2:32 TEV). Here is the flowering of the highest understanding that began to emerge among the prophets, to which Simeon was attuned, and to which the Gospel of Luke gave expression. The treasures that God had given to Israel were meant as a gift for all people. The glory of Israel was to be in making all its life a light to the Gentiles.

Simeon projected onto the infant Jesus what he and many like him had hoped for generations. He wished that what he had hoped would become reality during the lifetime of this infant. What Simeon said of this infant had been said of many infants, but when the life of Jesus took the shape and direction it did, then Simeon's words in reflection and retrospect became powerful and essential to Luke's biography of Jesus.

Simeon did not permit his excitement to become sugarcoated sentimentality as he celebrated what this "deliverer" would do. Simeon recognized the possible fate that would befall the deliverer. Maybe it was as he looked into the excited faces of Joseph and Mary that it hit him. Simeon's expression changed. He projected what he saw years into the future, but it was there so plainly that he could not pretend differently. "This child is chosen by God for the destruction and salvation of many in Israel . . . and sorrow, like a sharp sword, will break your own heart" (Lk. 2:34–35 TEV).

Was Simeon being contradictory to say the same person would be the salvation and destruction of many? Simeon knew enough about God and enough about people to know that if this infant was God's deliverer, then some would follow him and others would fight him. Incarnation, God coming to human beings through a human being, does not speak of only small and pleasant things. The baby Simeon saw became a man who would create the great schism that a shining, moral, and spiritual force always must make in human life. Some people loved this one whom Simeon blessed with the utmost devotion. They followed him to their death. Others hated him with as much intensity as those who loved him. The baby grew up. He both attracted and repelled people.

Simeon knew that if this baby became God's deliverer, his success would not be measured by the number of followers or the accumulation of wealth. Rather, the Anointed One of God maintains always and everywhere the sacred worth of human personality. Therefore, any policy or attitude in business or personal relationships that becomes obsessed with ideas and approaches that are relatively indifferent to the consequences of these on human lives is a repudiation of the spirit of God's Messiah.

Life has its element of tragedy and those who follow God's deliverer are not exempt. English clergyman William R. Inge noted that religion without tears is incongruent with the facts of life and the teaching of the New Testament.[11]

As Simeon held this baby on whom he pinned his hope and looked into the faces of his parents, he saw the agony that a deliverer and those who care about him would experience. Simeon would rather have bitten off his tongue than to have said what he did about sorrow, but in that holy place at that holy moment, he felt as though he had no choice. Then he handed the baby back to Mary and departed in something less than the perfect peace he had dreamed of all those long years of waiting.

Simeon is an old man about whom we know little. We would not know anything about him at all were it not for Luke. The theme of an old man anticipating the greatness of a child is not unique to the Bible. Such stories have been documented about Asita and the infant Buddha. Many years later, as the followers of Jesus remembered his life and their experience with him, they reflected on what it meant for him to be a deliverer. Perhaps it was in that context that Mary told Luke about Simeon. Then Luke, with his perceptive skill, wove together the personal meaning and universal application of Simeon's experience and response. Pervasive in Simeon's encounter as he holds the tiny baby and looks at Joseph and Mary is hope. Hope had sustained Simeon through all his years of waiting as one of the Quiet in the Land, even in the double-edged message that the Anointed One of God would cause destruction for some and deliverance for others. The note of hope rang clear and certain. Indeed, Simeon plays a vital supportive role as a servant of hope in the drama of all dramas, the drama of God coming to the world.

The Magi

Matthew said that magi came looking for Jesus. Magi and magician have the same root word, and that is unfortunate. Although magicians are entertaining and very skilled, they are skilled in illusion and deception, the hand being quicker than the eye.

Magi originally were a priestly caste among the Medes. They served the same function for the Medes that the Levites did for the Israelites. The Magi were recognized later as teachers of religion and science among the Medo-Persians with special interest in astrology and medicine. The Magi came to be identified as wise men through their roles as teachers.

Babylon, Mede, and Persia were east of Israel. There is nothing in the least improbable about the Magi traveling west from Babylon. They would find welcome audiences anywhere, from royal courts to market places. Expectation of some type of messiah was in the air almost everywhere during the first century.

The Magi came late to visit Jesus, perhaps as much as two years after his birth. There is nothing in Matthew's account of the story that tells how many Magi there were or that they were kings. Many have assumed that three people brought the gifts because Matthew identifies three types of gifts. Origen, one of the early church fathers, first suggested in the third century that there were three Magi. It was Tertullian, another church father in the second century, who first suggested that the Magi were kings. Later, the names of Melchior, Caspar, and Balthazar were given to these visitors. Three bodies were found in 1158 in the Church of St. Eustorgia near Milan. The bodies were presumed to be those of the Magi. When Emperor Frederick Barbarossa captured Milan, he took the bodies to Germany and deposited them in the Cologne Cathedral in 1164. The Shrine of the Three Kings of Cologne became a famous place of pilgrimage. It was visited by the wife of Bath in Chaucer's *Canterbury Tales.*

A custom developed in the Middle Ages for the rich and powerful to make offerings in church of gold, frankincense, and myrrh. The Queen of England continues this custom today. Twenty-five golden sovereigns are changed into notes and distributed to the aged poor, frankincense is given to the church to be used in worship, and myrrh is given to the hospital. Of course, the tradition of having the Magi be kings made nice symbolism to suggest that kings came to worship *the* king.

The gifts of the Magi—gold, frankincense, and myrrh—have developed symbolic meaning. Gold symbolized royalty, frankincense symbolized divinity, and myrrh symbolized humanity. These gifts were characteristic of that time, especially if the gifts were intended for a king.

The Magi went to Jerusalem and asked about the born king. They said they had seen his star rise in the East. The Magi were astrologers, people who observed and studied the stars. Apparently, some heavenly brilliance had spoken to the Magi that they interpreted as the entry of a king into the world. Halley's comet was visible in 11 B.C.E., and in 7 B.C.E., there was a brilliant conjunction of Saturn and Jupiter. There was an unusual astronomical phenomenon between 5 and 2 B.C.E. During those years, on the first day of the Egyptian month, Mesori, Sirius, the Dog Star, rose at sunrise and shone with extraordinary brilliance. The Egyptian word, Mesori, means birth of a prince.

Jesus was born sometime between 9 and 4 B.C.E. Dionysius Exiguus of Rome developed the Christian calendar in the sixth century. In doing his work, he failed to synchronize it with the Roman calendar. It has been historically documented that Herod the Great, who was the Roman assigned ruler of Judea, died in 4 B.C.E.

The word that Matthew used to refer to the one born king is the word for child; whereas, Luke's reference is to an infant. This suggests that Jesus was beyond one year of age when the Magi arrived in Jerusalem. A second indication that Jesus may have been a year or more old at this time was Herod's decree that all male children two years of age and younger in Bethlehem and its neighborhoods be killed. Herod was taking no chances in getting rid of one whom he feared would overtake his throne. An additional suggestion is that the Magi had no rapid transportation system to get them from Babylon or Persia to Jerusalem. They traveled by foot. That would imply that it would have been at least several months from the time they saw the star and when they arrived in Jerusalem. Since they were students of the stars, I doubt that they took off on a trip at the first sign of an unusual astronomical formation. Rather, they studied the formation long enough to conclude that it had not been an astrological mirage or a visual slight of sight.

Herod solicited the help of the Magi in locating this child born king. He requested their aid under the pretense that he, too, wished to worship him. For some reason, the Magi did not believe Herod was being honest about his intentions. Possibly, Herod's reputation had preceded him. Perhaps it was the urgency with which Herod had sought them when they arrived in Jerusalem and were asking questions rather than the Magi having sought Herod. Maybe it was through their encounter with Herod that they sensed insincerity and were suspicious of Herod's motives. Whatever the reason or reasons for their suspicions, they were focused in a dream in which the Magi concluded they should go home from Bethlehem by another road rather than traveling through Jerusalem. Herod was furious when he realized what had happened. That was when he sent out the murder decree and put a price on the head of every two-year-old and younger boy living in and around Bethlehem.

With Herod expressing this kind of furor, Joseph dreamed of a place of safety for his family. They packed their things and headed for Egypt. They remained there until Herod died. They then returned to Israel and, as Matthew told the story, it seems as though they were on their way to Bethlehem when Joseph learned that Archelaus had succeeded his father as Rome's ruler of Judea. Joseph decided to bypass Bethlehem and Judea as places to live and went to Nazareth in Galilee, where he and the family settled down.

The birth and manifestation of Jesus are essential in the doctrine of the Incarnation, the enfleshment of God, or how God came to dwell as completely as possible in a human being. Dale Moody, professor of theology at the Southern Baptist Theological Seminary, identified Jesus as a man full of God.

Several scholars, including Frank Stagg and Douglas R. A. Hare, suggest that the Magi were Gentiles because they requested to see the child born king of the Jews. Therefore, their visit to see Jesus represented that God dwelling in the human flesh of Jesus was a God for all people and that there was to be neither Greek nor Jew. God made no distinctions between people on the basis of pedigree. Whether or not that is implied in the question of the Magi, certainly, in all that we know about God from what was revealed throughout the life of Jesus, this equality of all people before God is true. Jesus truly was a person full of God, a person for all seasons, and a person for all reasons who portrayed the love of God. Matthew's story of the visit of the Magi to Jerusalem and Bethlehem in search of the one born king, whose star the Magi had seen rise in the East, has given the Magi a supportive role in the drama of God coming to the world.

There is a story from Kierkegaard about a king who loved his people dearly, but was dissatisfied with the relationship he had with them. He wanted to share with his subjects and invited them to come to the palace. He even sent out messengers to encourage such encounters, but the people were timid, afraid, and unwilling. At last, to the dismay and concern of everyone in his court, the king laid aside his royal robes and donned the garb of a peasant and went to live among his people as one of them. At first, the people did not recognize him, but when it began to dawn on them who was among them, they began to share with him in ways they had never done before. His willingness to move toward the people proved how the king really felt about his people. It also made possible a bond of closeness that nothing else could have achieved.

The miracle of Christmas is that long before the king Kierkegaard mentions went to live among his people, God had moved to live among the people of the world. God continues to search for and reach out to people through people. God seeks to come where we are so we will know and receive God's love and grace. Christmas was God's idea. The drama of God coming to the world is played out through the lives of Mary, Joseph, Jesus, Elizabeth, Herod, the innkeeper, Simeon, and the Magi. And every time that people welcome God into their lives, the drama is reenacted.

QUESTIONS TO PONDER

1. With which of the leading cast members in the drama of God coming to the world do you most identify? Why?

2. With which of the supporting cast in the drama of God coming to the world do you most identify? Why?

3. What does it mean to you to be favored of God?

4. How does Bailey's information about a "typical Middle Eastern" home affect the meaning and value of the Christmas story for you?

5. What influence do you think Joseph had on Jesus' development?

6. How was Jesus' understanding of the image of God influenced by Mary? by Joseph?

7. What is your understanding and explanation of Simeon saying that the same person would lead to the salvation and destruction of many?

8. How is God continuing the drama of coming to the world in your life?

4

WHAT SHALL WE CALL JESUS?
PHILIPPIANS 2:1–11

Several years ago we were visiting my wife's aunt in Florida. We had been talking for a while over dinner when she looked across the table at us and asked, "Where did you get such dumb names for your kids?" Apparently she had given no consideration to the unusual names in her family including Barney, Bink, and Roland.

I mentioned in the previous chapter that one of the first tasks of parents, including Jesus' parents, is to give names to their children. Naming children is the beginning process of their identity, and the lives they live give shape, meaning, and interpretation to their names.

Unique in God coming to the world is that God continues to come to the world. God comes to us in our generation. People in each generation are invited to participate in naming the One born long ago in Bethlehem who uniquely comes to us and is born in us in the cities and towns where we live. Joseph and Mary named their infant son several days after his birth. They called him Jesus.

Because God cared enough to send the very best, wrapped in human flesh, and because God continues to come to the world and to come to us, we have the opportunity and privilege to name this One who comes to us. Each of us participates in the naming. As God comes to you, what will you call this One who comes to you?

A name is important. According to the Genesis account, Adam was instructed to name the animals according to their nature. The animals' names were labels for identification. These names assisted in the ordering of the creation. Too often we use names only as labels of identification.

A name in biblical thought is not merely a label of identification; it expresses the essential nature of the one named. The name denotes the essential being, and in Hebrew thought nothing exists unless it has a name.

Like Joseph and Mary, we are invited to name the One born in Bethlehem. Many suggestions are available, but we need to choose a name that reflects the nature of this One who came so long ago and continues to come and influence lives this very moment. What shall we call him? Let's call him Lord, Shepherd, Savior, and King.

LORD

"Lord" has a variety of meanings. Lord was used in antiquity as an adjective long before it was used as a noun. In its adjectival context, *kurios*, the Greek word translated as "Lord," means having power, being empowered, competent, or decisive. As a noun, the word was used as early as the first half of the fourth century B.C.E. and, at that time, it had two fixed meanings. The first meaning was "as the lawful owner of a slave." The second meaning was that of "legal guardian of a wife or child."

The word Lord is used in the New Testament in a variety of references. It can refer to the owner of slaves and property. *Kurios* is used to refer to the owner of the vineyard in Matthew's Gospel. Lord is one who has the power and ability to dispose of something or someone.

God as Lord is an ancient concept. This concept is reflected in the 97th Psalm. Through numerous poems, the psalmists express their conclusion that, in order to rule, God must be present. For them, the converse also is true. Chaos and anarchy prevail when or if God is absent.

Paul continues with the concept of God as Lord in his letters. The second chapter of Philippians is Paul's version of the Christmas story. The passage has been identified as a hymn and could be seen as Paul's Christmas carol in which he stresses the importance of "the name above every name."

People are named during infancy, usually before any distinguishing characteristic has been identified. The name given to an infant usually says much more about the one naming than the one named. Consider your name. At your birth it reflected more about your parents than about you. What you have done with your life has given meaning and character to your name. Only as an infant grows through childhood and adolescence into adulthood can one see the trends in that person's life. Rare is the person who can take those trends and formulate a name that captures the essence of the person. The closest we get to doing that is with nicknames. However, as people develop, their traits become identified with their names. Thus, certain names have come to have specific meanings.

According to Paul, God gave Jesus a name above every name. God bestowed this name on Jesus at the end of the journey rather than at the beginning. Perhaps God was attempting to capture the whole of Jesus' life in one name so the name and the life would be synonymous.

Paul quickly summarized the life of Jesus leading to the name given him by God. Jesus, who had the essence of God, did not view equality with God as something to be held onto at all risks and hazards. The equality was a possession he could lay aside. Not only did he choose to lay aside his equality with God, but he also chose to become a slave. Jesus was limited by time, space, and power. He faced weariness, hunger, and other common human struggles and needs. He needed friends. He suffered with those who suffered and rejoiced with those rejoicing. Choosing to be a servant, Jesus poured out his life entirely to meet the needs of people. He gave all that he was. He gave himself. He lay aside all opportunities to be God. He sought to be obedient to God and made himself vulnerable to people. He died a criminal's death not because God demanded it, but because people demanded it. Paul concluded that Jesus lived what he taught.

The climax to this version of the Christmas story is "God gave him a name above every name." But what was that name? There are many candidates: Jesus, Jesus Christ, Dignity, Honor, and Lord. Jesus is a popular choice because it is used in Philippians 2:10 following Paul's statement about the name above every name; however, this choice is doubtful because he was known as Jesus from birth. Lord is used in Philippians 2:11 to refer to Jesus. Paul says every knee should bow and every tongue confess, not that Jesus Christ is Jesus, but that Jesus Christ is Lord. The name Lord means to have power, to rule, to bring order by one's presence. The name above every name given to Jesus is Lord and it represents the whole person that Jesus was, is, and ever shall be. What are you going to call him? Call him Lord.

SHEPHERD

One person often has many relationships in life. A person may be known as a daughter, a sister, an aunt, a mother, a grandmother, a sister-in-law, a wife, and a friend. How another person is related to this woman determines which relationship is prominent, but that does not negate the other relationships.

God comes to each generation and the Son of God is born in each generation. Although we may visit the ancient story and traditions surrounding the Bethlehem event, we are invited to participate in the naming process of this One born long ago and born again in our lives. Whether we name this One or not will not alter who he is, but the name(s) we give him will reveal who he is to us. Let's call him Shepherd!

Apparently, civilization began in the Fertile Crescent of the Mesopotamian Valley. In the prebiblical days of the ancient orient, the king was described as the shepherd appointed by the deity. His task was to look after the needs of the people. Early Egyptian writings identify gods bearing the title of Shepherd.

The term "shepherd" later came to mean one who herds sheep. The people of antiquity were nomadic, wandering people on the move. They traveled from place to place with the animals they had domesticated looking for food and water for themselves and their flocks. The basis of the economy in Palestine during the biblical period included tending flocks and cultivating small crops. The arid region required that herds of sheep, goats, and cattle be moved from place to place and remain in isolated areas for long stretches of time because that's where the grass and water were. These areas often would be far from the dwelling place of the owner. Jacob's sons were shepherding his flock some distance from home. Joseph apparently traveled a long distance to where they were. Herding the flocks was an independent, responsible, and dangerous job.

By the time of Jesus' birth, hired shepherds did much of the shepherding. Difficulties arose with the hired help. Frequently, in the threat of danger or personal harm, the hired shepherd would flee the flock to save his own life. Because the flock was not his, often the hired shepherd would sacrifice his job rather than attempt to save the flock.

The ancient Hebrew Scriptures clearly portray shepherding as an admirable profession. However, by the time of Jesus' birth, shepherds were despised. Because they could not maintain the cleanliness requirements, shepherds were forbidden to worship in the Temple. They were unclean because of vocation and treated as outcasts. The shepherd is included in the rabbinical lists of thieving and cheating occupations. Like the publicans or tax collectors, shepherds were deprived of civil rights; they could not fulfill a judicial office or be admitted in court as witnesses. Discrimination against shepherds was based on the assumption that a shepherd would be tempted to steal some of the increase of the flock. People were forbidden to buy wool, milk, or a kid from a shepherd on the assumption that it was stolen property. Shepherds were guilty until proven innocent.

Although shepherds became despised in daily life, the ancient Hebrew Scriptures hold up the shepherd as a metaphor for God. Exactly when the description of God as shepherd became implanted in Israel's understanding is unclear. Whatever the order of events that led to this understanding, the shepherd image of God is embedded in the living piety of Israel and recorded in scripture. God is depicted as the shepherd who goes ahead of the flock (Ps. 68:7), guides the flock, leads the flock to pastures, finds places of rest for the flock, protects the flock (Ps. 23:2–4; Jer. 50:19), and whistles to the dispersed to gather them (Zech. 10:8). Describing God as the shepherd of Israel underscores the conviction that God shelters Israel.

The New Testament, in contrast to the rabbinical writings, never judges the shepherd adversely. In the gospels, the sacrificial loyalty of the shepherd is depicted with loving sympathy. The shepherds are portrayed as models for living because the shepherds know their animals, call them by name, seek the lost, celebrate finding the lost, and hazard their own lives to protect the flock.

Although God is never called a shepherd in the New Testament, the shepherd metaphor is a picture of God. The joy of the shepherd when he finds his sheep after a difficult search is conveyed in the parables that Jesus used to illustrate the relationship of God to people. Jesus justified his association with the outcast of culture saying it was like the boundless joy of the rejoicing shepherd in the parable when he brought back a sheep that had been lost.

The shepherd analogy was one of the more popular ones when referring to God. Psalm 23 is the best-known passage of scripture that refers to God as the shepherd. No doubt Jesus had this psalm in mind when he referred to himself as the "Good Shepherd." The Hebrew people enjoyed taking a familiar image borrowed from ordinary life and meditating on the various ways it might be analogous to realities in the spiritual realm.

The characteristics of the "good shepherd" are implied in the 23rd Psalm. Certainly God is more than a shepherd and people more than sheep, but the psalmist used the shepherd-sheep analogy because it communicated so clearly to the Hebrew people. Even today, it is common in Israel to see a shepherd in a valley or along a hillside with a herd of sheep walking with him. While the imagery has little or no meaning to us who are a generation or two away from the rural setting and culture, there are characteristics of the shepherd that are descriptive of God. Jesus explicitly identified the characteristics of caregiving and life-giving as evidence of the good shepherd.

The opening line of Psalm 23 states immediately that relating to God is like having a shepherd who supplies every need. Characteristic of the good shepherds is they look out for the welfare of the sheep, making sure the sheep have what they need to survive. The good shepherd cares for the sheep.

Jesus used the word "good" to modify the shepherd and to imply that there was a difference and distinction between good and bad shepherds. The word that is translated "good" in John's Gospel (10:11) describes a quality of winsomeness and attractiveness that makes being a shepherd a lovely thing.

Actually, the distinction that Jesus made in his reference to the shepherd was between the good shepherd and the hired man. The shepherd is invested in the welfare of the flock. The herd belongs to him. He has ownership in the herd. His entire livelihood is at stake, and he will take risks to keep the sheep from harm, to be certain their needs are met and, if one gets lost, he goes in search of the lost sheep once the rest of the flock is safely in the sheepfold. This remains the case today wherever there is an owner of sheep. In February 1987, a flock of sheep in the western part of the United States became frightened and was headed toward their death. The owner, at great risk to himself, diverted the attention of many of the sheep. He lost two hundred sheep because they plunged over a cliff, but he managed, because of his effort, to keep eight hundred from following the same path as the two hundred.

The hired man, whom Jesus contrasted to the shepherd, will not risk his life for the sheep because his only investment is a day's wages. Thus, when something threatening arises, the hired man easily and quickly takes his leave because he has little to lose. Jesus said that the good shepherd would lay down his life for his sheep. This was an original contribution of Jesus to the understanding of the role of the good shepherd. Willingness to give one's life for the sheep is the height of care for the benefit of the sheep. At another time Jesus drew the parallel to his relationship with people when he said, "Greater love has no man than this, that a man lay down his life for his friends" (Jn. 15:13 RSV). Jesus was a caring, loving friend who took great risks for the benefit of human beings. He was concerned that those who came to him would be nourished and nurtured so that they could and would care for others and be willing to lay down their lives in love for the benefit of others.

The characteristic of caring for and giving of oneself for the benefit of others is demonstrated by the good shepherd who guides, guards, and gathers together those under his care. The psalmist suggests that God provides for his every need, and then enumerates what those needs are: food, drink, renewed strength, and guidance down the right paths. Jesus, as the good shepherd, saw one of his major responsibilities to guide people to the source of nourishment, renewed strength, and righteousness. Jesus was concerned with the physical needs of all people, and he was concerned that people not confuse these means of living with the ends of life. People are forever making this mistake and overdosing on the means of life. This mistake leads to gluttony, obesity, addictions, substance abuse, greed, taking, grabbing, clinging. People become locked in fear, insecure, and unsure of themselves. They attempt to fill their emptiness and loneliness with things or they use things and substances—drugs, alcohol, work, and pleasure—to kill the pain of their emptiness and loneliness. Jesus, as the good shepherd, seeks to lead us in directions that will nourish and enrich our lives. We need to spend more time in thought, meditation, and communicating with God to discover what it is that God wants to give us. This is the direction in which Jesus, the good shepherd, is guiding us.

The good shepherd also serves as a guard, a protector of our lives. The shepherd is a protector in the sense of journeying ahead of the sheep and standing between them and anything that might destroy them—wild animals, a deep crevice, or a tight place that would trap them. The psalmist understood this responsibility of the shepherd and transferred this to God as the shepherd who would journey with people in the valley of the shadow of death and would prepare a banquet table in the presence of enemies. Both situations might evoke fear from the traveler, except that the presence of God as the good shepherd would displace the fear. As a protector and guard, the good shepherd does not serve as a body snatcher, jerking people out of difficult situations like a firefighter in a rescue operation. Rather, God seeks to be present with people throughout their lives and certainly when they face their most difficult, life-threatening situations, like walking in the valley of the shadow of death, God is with them, comforting and caring for them. Psalm 139 states emphatically that there is nowhere a person can go and be out of the presence of God. God desires to journey with us anywhere and everywhere we go, not as a tagalong, not as a nosey invader of privacy, but as one who loves and cares for us in all our circumstances.

In addition to guiding and guarding us, Jesus seeks to gather us together as one flock, to unite us as one people. Zechariah 11:6 suggests that the characteristic of a false shepherd is when no effort is made to gather together the scattered sheep. There are those who seem intent on actively scattering those who desire to follow Christ. We have seen it, heard it, and felt it in rabid denominationalism advocated by many. People have pitted one group against another. Nothing is further from the purpose and effort of the good shepherd who said there is one shepherd and one flock, but not one fold. Jesus said there are other sheep not of this fold. We need to hear that, let it soak into our minds and hearts, and bear witness that we are followers of the good shepherd and make no decisions or judgments about anyone else with regard to their following the good shepherd. That is God's domain, not ours. Jesus said that the sheep hear the shepherd's voice, recognize their shepherd, come to the shepherd, and become one flock with one shepherd.

Many years ago, there was a missionary who was developing a friendship with the Indians in Saskatchewan. He referred to God as "Our Father," which was a new approach to the Indian chief who said he had never thought of the Great Spirit as Father. He said they referred to God as "thunder," "lightning," and "blizzard," and all of these analogies made them afraid. But "Our Father" was a beautiful expression to him. Then he asked, "Did you say you refer to God as your father?" The missionary nodded affirmatively. Next he asked, "Did you say that God also is the Father of the Indians?" and the missionary said, "Yes." Excitedly, the Indian chief responded, "Then you and I are brothers." The good shepherd draws people together as one people.

Jesus brought insight and understanding about relationship and access to God to which people had been blind and deaf for centuries. The way Jesus related to God was not a new way in the sense that the way had never been available before, but it was new in the sense that no one had ever done it this way before. Those are seven deadly words that immobilize and paralyze us: "We never did it that way before."

Jesus said that all who had preceded him were thieves and robbers. To whom was he referring? Surely he was not referring to Moses and the prophets because he often identified with Moses and he read from Isaiah when he began his ministry. He was not referring to John the Baptist, because he expressed high regard for him and even insisted that John baptize him. Apparently, the reference to thieves and robbers was to any person or group that sought to exploit people rather than serve them. It may have been a reference to some of the Pharisees who tried to take everything away from the beggar who had been cured of his blindness. In their blindness, on another level, the Pharisees sought to take away the welcome of the blind man's parents, the legitimacy of the cure that had occurred, and the fellowship of the synagogue community. Jesus' reference also may have been to some of the Sadducean and priestly authorities who controlled the Temple establishment that Jesus compared to a den of robbers (Mk. 11:17). They were depriving those who weren't Jews of opportunities to worship God. Jesus' statement also may have been a reference to some of the Zealots who resorted to deception and violence for religious purposes. Thieves and robbers were anybody who obstructed people from experiencing God's love and grace.

His statement also may refer to us. We, too, are thieves and robbers anytime we seek to exclude people from the care and love of the good shepherd. I think the most difficult thing to unlearn is exclusiveness. Anytime that people conclude that they are specially privileged, it is difficult for them to realize that the privileges they thought belonged only to them are open to all people. There have been occasions when we attempted to define how and when a relationship with God was initiated and developed. We have concluded that if others did not have an experience with God like ours, then their experience was not authentic. When this is our attitude, we are thieves and robbers, taking away from people a basic ingredient in the development of meaning in their lives. There are times when we speak of ourselves in the West, and especially in the United States, as though we have a corner on God's action and activity, implying with arrogance that others' experiences with God are less than ours. At those times, we are thieves and robbers.

No matter what Jesus taught through his ministry, the debate continued to rage between those scandalized by his intimacy with God and those impressed by his works of power. No one seemed ready to reevaluate the religious leadership in Judaism and ask if it was really protecting the people of God from their deadliest foes.

Jesus must have had the 23rd Psalm in mind when he talked about being the good shepherd. He took the characteristic of the shepherd as a caretaker a step beyond what anyone had considered it when he said that the good shepherd was one who would willingly lay down his life for the benefit and well-being of others. Certainly the way that Jesus went about his ministry exemplified the responsibilities of the shepherd as one caring for people by seeking to guide, guard, and gather people together, once suggesting that the gathering was like a hen gathering her chicks together. Jesus said that all of this was possible because people would hear and recognize his voice and come to him as one people. Have people heard the voice of Christ through the centuries in the lives of others, through the words of scripture, through the text of hymns, through meditation and communion with God, and through placing themselves in the context of worship? Having their blind eyes and deaf ears opened, they have discovered in Jesus the best illustration of what it means to be human, to relate to God, and to serve others as representatives of God. Jesus, as shepherd, was powerful imagery for those in the first century, and it continues to appeal to us in the twenty-first century. Consider the name "Shepherd" as you seek to name this One born long ago and born again in each generation. What shall we call him? Call him Shepherd.

SAVIOR

A common concern in all religions is salvation. Every religion may be described as an attempt at a way of salvation. Salvation has a primary position in religion regardless of how primitive or sophisticated the religious development is. In some sense, salvation is the ultimate concern of all religion. Salvation means to deliver, to redeem, or to recover property that has fallen into alien hands. It also means to have space enough to get away from doing evil.

Salvation is a process by which God delivers a person out of harm's way into safety, out of slavery into freedom, out of fragmentation into wholeness. The work of God as deliverer is like that of an obstetrician. The obstetrician cannot keep an expectant mother from pain. The pain can be deadened, but it cannot be taken away. The way out is the way through. The obstetrician is there to aid the mother and go with her through the pain of childbirth. I recall reading a story in *The Pulpit Digest* about a Scottish plowboy-martyr who said to a fellow sufferer as the end of life drew ghastly near, "God never guaranteed to keep us out of troubles, but he did promise to bring us through the worst of them. And he will do it."

Salvation is approached in an unusual and unique manner in the Bible. God is portrayed as savior. God is Noah's savior and will be the savior of all who will join Noah. The children of Israel developed their belief that God was their savior as a result of the Exodus. Moses embodied the living God in flesh and blood, but God was the deliverer and savior. The saving event of the Exodus is reenacted today by Jewish people. It is made contemporary in the dramatic representation of the Passover meal. The saving event is a fact of the past that lives in the present. In this way, God has been savior, is now savior, and always will be savior.

The biblical material proclaims the fact of salvation. The salvation and redemption of people is always through people. God redeems people by people. Woven throughout the biblical accounts of God's activity and involvement with people is the fact that God actually has in concrete historical fact saved people from destruction. Thus, the approach of the biblical writers is that the historical salvation is only a preview of the salvation that is to come. Whether a historical fact or a preview of things to come, salvation always comes from God, by God, and through God as a gift to people. God is the one who saves. Thus, we can call God Savior.

Salvation is grounded eternally in who God is. God's purpose from the foundation of the world has been for people to be drawn to God. God and people are brought together most clearly in Jesus of Nazareth. What God does in Christ is not anything different than what God had been doing all along. Salvation occurred for people throughout history, as they were willing to respond to God's loving presence. What happened in and through Jesus' life was an extension and intensification of what God already was doing. What the gospels affirm is that in the presence of Christ, people were radically changed. The change was so radical that it was described as being new life. This new existence is the will and desire of God for everybody.

The name Jesus is especially significant for Matthew. He sees the name suggesting that deliverance and salvation spring from Yahweh. Matthew adds that his name was Jesus because he would deliver people from their sins. This was a corrective to the Zealot notion that the Anointed One would save Israel from Roman rule.

To name the Bethlehem baby Jesus is to announce that God is salvation. To make that announcement is to align ourselves with the one who delivers. To align ourselves with God is to identify ourselves as the saving, redeeming people of God. This means salvation has begun for us and in us, but the deliverance is not complete. The process has started. We are saved from destroying ourselves and saved to become God incarnate. God has been coming through the centuries to people through people. God desires to take on flesh and blood again; God wants to be born again in the world through you and me. Will we make room for God? Will we invite God to be born in us? If we do, what shall we call this One being born in us? Call him Savior, because this One will show us the way. This One will deliver us from harm to safety, from bondage to freedom, from fragmentation to wholeness, and from selfishness to selflessness. Anyone who will deliver us from all of this deserves to be called Savior.

KING

I've never met a king, have you? Most of us have seen a king or a queen on television. We have seen King Hussein of Jordan and Queen Elizabeth of England. Many people around the world attended the royal wedding of Prince Charles and Lady Diana in 1981 by way of television. But few people ever meet kings or queens.

More important than having the opportunity to meet a king or a queen is being able to recognize royalty. If you were told that a king or queen was coming to your home today, how would you recognize the monarch? Would it be the limousine in which he would be riding or would it be the jewel-studded clothing she would be wearing? How would you recognize royalty?

If a king or queen were coming to your house today, how would you dress to greet royalty? Would you wear the very best outfit you have? Would you have to buy a new outfit because nothing you own would be appropriate?

What if the visiting monarch had done some checking on you and learned that when you are relaxing at home you wear cutoff jeans, a ragged T-shirt, and no shoes? Desiring to be at ease and to fit in, what if a king appeared at your door dressed like he thought you would be dressed? Would you recognize him or usher him away so the door would not be blocked when real royalty arrived? Perhaps this king would gladly be ushered away because he was looking for someone who would be an authentic human being rather than someone trying to impress him by putting his best foot forward.

To read Hebrew Scripture is to discover reigning royalty as a central issue. Israel viewed the king as God's Anointed One. Wherever life was in shambles, the people looked to the king as the One through whom God would work to make life better for them. Isaiah 11 describes the ideal king. He had a living king in mind. With a hopefulness that repeated disillusionment failed to diminish, the Jews hailed every new king as the Lord's Anointed One who would usher in a golden age. Isaiah paints a picture of a perfect, just, and equitable government that this king will bring to pass:

> He shall not judge by what his eyes see,
>   or decide by what his ears hear;
> but with righteousness he shall judge the poor,
>   and decide with equity for the meek of the earth;
> and he shall smite the earth with the rod of his mouth,
>   and with the breath of his lips he shall slay the wicked.
>
> (Isa. 11:3b–4 RSV)

Isaiah says that when God is the reigning royalty in people's lives, there is a revolutionary peace that transforms their lives. Words like these from Isaiah shatter our images of royalty.

Is this what God does to us, shatters our images of how we have portrayed God and what we expect God to be like? Our image of God too often is like Boss Godfrey in the movie *Cool Hand Luke*. Godfrey wears mirrored sunglasses so no one can see his eyes. His face always is expressionless and he never speaks. Godfrey carries a walking stick that he beats against his leg as he walks along the pavement supervising the chain gang. His rifle is always near as a reminder that he has absolute power of life and death over the gang. For too many people God is like Boss Godfrey, one whose eyes are hidden and who dispassionately and arbitrarily sets the limits on people's lives.

The Christmas drama tells us God is much different than this. The image of God is shattered because God never looks quite as we expect. Several years ago, I finally met a woman face-to-face whom I had talked to several times by telephone. Upon meeting me, she said with surprise, "So you are Howard Roberts! You don't look like I expected!" She thought my voice was older than my face. I assured her that they are both the same age. God's appearances never come quite as we had expected and even in our great expectation of God's coming, we are surprised.

Part of the surprise is that God comes wrapped in human flesh. The surprise is intensified in the kind of flesh in which God dresses. Reigning royalty came as a paltry peasant. Jesus grew up as a poor boy among poor people. His ministry always was to the enslaved, the poverty-stricken, the imprisoned, the sick, and the outcast.

God came as a stranger and a foreigner. Jesus' parents went to a strange town at the time of his birth. His first bed was a manger, the bed of a visitor at best. His family fled to Egypt where they were strangers and sojourners. They were regarded as strangers when they returned to Nazareth. As Jesus began his ministry, he felt isolation from the Pharisees. Later he was arrested as a stranger, tried as a foreigner, killed as an outcast, and buried in a borrowed tomb.

When we look for royalty, we search the palaces. We go where the power and money are, but royalty is not there. Jesus inverted the royalty system and shattered the image of authentic royalty. Jesus said, by word and life, if you want to find royalty, look at the servant. When we search for royalty, we expect that the more servants a person has waiting on her, the more regal she is. Jesus said royalty is in the Samaritan, the tax collector, the leper, the woman at the well.

John the Baptist said, "Prepare the way of the Lord" (Mt. 3:3 RSV). What we have failed to hear in that exhortation is that we need to get ready to meet God in every face and hear God in every voice. What is shattering is that the dirtier the face and the more foul the voice, the closer we are to royalty as far as Jesus is concerned. A Swedish proverb says, "God often goes about in worn-out shoes."

In his poem "How the Great Guest Came," Edwin Markham tells the story of Conrad the Cobbler who dreamed the Lord was coming to visit him. He washed the walls and shelves of his shop, decorated it with branches of holly and fir, and put milk, honey, and bread on the table. He sat down to wait, thinking how kindly he would treat the Lord when he arrived.

He looked out the window as he sat waiting and saw a barefoot beggar walking in the rain. He went to the door, called the beggar in, and gave him a pair of shoes. Later he saw an old woman, bent and worn, struggling with a heavy load of firewood. He gave her some food and helped her on her way. The poem goes:

Then to his door came a little child, Lost and afraid in a world
    so wild,
In the big, dark world. Catching him up,
He gave him the milk in the waiting cup,
And led him home to his mother's arms,
Out of the reach of the world's alarms.
Now it was evening and the old shoemaker still waited.
    Had the Lord forgotten to come? he wondered sadly.
Then soft in the silence a voice he heard:
"Lift up your heart, for I kept my word.
Three times I came to your friendly door;
Three times my shadow was on your floor;
I was the beggar with the bruised feet;
I was the woman you gave food to eat;
I was the child on the homeless street!"[1]

In naming the One born long ago and born again in our lives, we need to recognize him in order to name him. The news that frightened Herod was that there was one born king. Herod was king by force, manipulation, and coercion. But the one born king is the one who has the innate ability to rule.

We can call him King because of what we know of his nature. His wisdom and tenderness reveal a person of perfect psychological balance. He spoke sternly against adultery, but dealt tenderly and mercifully with the adulteress. He opposed exploitation of people, but he ate dinner with Zacchaeus and invited Matthew to be a disciple. Both were tax collectors and scripture indicts them as exploiters of others. We can call "King" one who deals so forcefully with issues and so lovingly with people.

We can call Christ King because of the way he defined himself as king. Many wanted to pin meaning onto the name of King for Jesus, but he refused to permit others to define his task or his identity. He did that for himself. Jesus refused to be the military leader that many associated with being a king. He sought to bring change in people's lives by joining with them at their invitation. He went about changing lives nonviolently, but violence often surrounded him and finally destroyed him. In the midst of all of that, he never lost sight of his objective to give life in its fullness and never did he attempt to force his way onto others. To call Christ King is to give ourselves obediently to one whose nature shows us the love, mercy, understanding, and acceptance of God.

To call Christ King is to identify ourselves as servants. We are servants because we choose to be. As servants, we feed the hungry, clothe the naked, and visit the imprisoned. If we do these things because these people are Christ to us, then we are coming in the wise men's spirit to do the wise men's act.

As you think of the One born centuries ago in Bethlehem, as you recall much of what has been said about him, as you examine what you need in your life, how you identify this One born long ago and desiring to be born again in you will shape how you see yourself, how you relate to God and to the world. God is coming to us and now is near us, wrapped as a human being. Consider what you will call this One who comes to you now. Call him Lord, call him Shepherd, call him Savior, call him King!

QUESTIONS TO PONDER

1. What is the significance of a name?

2. Is there any significance in the names used to identify the God who comes to you?

3. What do the terms Lord, Shepherd, Savior, and King mean to you?

4. How do these terms communicate something of the nature of God to you?

5. What terms would you use to identify what God is like?

5

WHAT SHALL WE BE?

1 JOHN 1:1–10

To become involved in the naming process is to get tied up with identity. Who we are and who we become are affected by what we call the One born long ago in Bethlehem and born again in us. To answer the question, "What shall we call him?" raises another question, "What shall we be?" We are to become the incarnation of God by being children of promise, prophets of mercy, makers of peace, and conductors of love.

CHILDREN OF PROMISE

A theologian once said that the Christian, rather than viewing life as encircled and choked by hostile forces, sees it instead as "filled with the air of promises which hardly anyone hears." What good is a world of promises when what we really need is a cure for cancer, a redistribution of resources so that people everywhere have enough, a breakthrough in Middle East hostilities, and practical insights which can break the impasse in human relationships at home and at work? We will take an answer to any one of these over a handful of promises.

Yet, promises are a significant part of our daily lives. Have you thought how much of your life is built on promises? Consider the promise of friendship. The offer of a relationship does not guarantee anything. If you promise to be my friend, the world of power politics, tragic accidents, leukemia, and death is not touched at all. There is nothing in your promise of friendship that will protect me from any of these or reduce my vulnerability to the devastation that any of these might have in my life. What about the difficulties you have in your life—family conflict, stress, monthly bills? Does the promise of friendship solve any of these problems? The most we can get from each other is the promise of friendship, a promise that we care about each other's difficulties in the struggles in life. We promise to be fellow strugglers as we somehow "muddle through" some or all of this.

If this is all we can expect from the promise of friendship, do we then throw away the relationship and negate the promise? Will we say instead, "Give me some real answers, solve some problems, never mind these promises of friendship, we need something that will do us some good"? Of course not, because even in our deepest longing for hard solutions, we have learned that the promise of friendship in all the solitary places of our lives is more valuable than even a cure for leukemia. All the cures and answers in the world are worthless without people who care about us.

Biblical religion is delicately balanced on a promise. Through many people and various events, the promise is the same: "I will be your God, if you will be my people." That is *all* there is. The only guarantee in this promise is the assurance of a relationship. There is no protection in this promise: no protection from drought, from enslavement, from torture and persecution, no protection from hatred and violence and crucifixion, no protection from family conflict and dissolution, no protection from bankruptcy, no protection from malignancy or malignant attitudes and actions. This promise of God does not say life will be fair or just.

Through the centuries people have rushed to altars, shrines, temples, synagogues, cathedrals, and church buildings seeking protection. Maybe you have gone to church at some time in your life expecting, even demanding, protection from the erosion or devastation that events were having on your life. If you have, you have probably been disappointed because your expectations were not met. God does not and cannot guarantee protection. God does offer a relationship that begins and ends in a promise: "I will be your God if you will be my people."

According to the psalmist (Ps. 106:24), the root sin of Israel was discontent with God's promise. The essence of their hope was their confidence in God's promise (Ps. 18:30; 119:38). Hope and confidence in God's promise permeate the ninth chapter of Isaiah. The coronation of every king stirred the hope that the promise of God would be fully embodied in the new king. Whenever the promise of God is embodied in a human being, that person will relate with justice and fairness. Every king disappointed the Israelites because no king lived out the promise. If the Jews had cherished protection rather than promise, they would have hailed many messiahs.

John caught a glimpse of the promise or, maybe, the promise caught him. He was swept away. Read the first eighteen verses of John's Gospel. It is a breathtaking opening. St. Teresa once complained, "I wish only that I could write with both hands, so as not to forget one thing while I am saying another." John gives the impression he was thinking much faster than he could write. The rush of staggering assertions overwhelms the reader's mind. One would like to pause and take it all in but is swept along by the rush of expressions. Something very big, but indescribable, something that will not go into words is being written about here.

Later, as people in the early church continued to get hold of God's promise, they found the promise had hold of them. They found Isaiah's words to be expressive and descriptive of this indescribable promise. The church has used Isaiah's words to communicate the promise for centuries: "For to us a child is born, to us a son is given and his name will be called Wonderful Counselor, the Mighty God, the Everlasting Father, the Prince of Peace" (Isa. 9:6 RSV).

Advent is a season of worship for the church to celebrate the promise of God to come to people and to come through people to people. It is the celebration of the indescribable promise expressed in Jesus of Nazareth and the invitation to all people everywhere to become children of the promise. An eleventh-century Hasidic rabbi said, "Human beings are God's language."

Of course there are two parts to the promise. Both are necessary. A promise is made, and it must be received. Refusal to receive the promise nullifies it. It keeps it incomplete. God's promise to be our God can only be completed if we are willing to be God's people. Willingness to be God's people results in God being our God.

Closing my eyes to the sunlight does not make the world dark. It only shuts the light out from my life. Responsiveness is necessary in order for the light of promise to shine in our lives. There were villages where Jesus wrought amazing things during his ministry. There were other villages where little, if anything, happened because the people set their minds to be unresponsive. People may go to hear a comedienne. She may be the funniest person ever to step on stage. But if a person in the audience has decided that he will not laugh, nothing the comedienne says or does will evoke a response of laughter. So it is for people and God's promise. There are those who are unresponsive. They refuse to accept the promise.

Nathaniel struggled with the promise. He said God's promise was important and necessary, but he didn't think it would take root and grow in Nazareth. He could not foresee anything good coming out of Nazareth. If not Nathaniel, someone else may have exclaimed, "Mighty works! Not he! I knew him as a boy. I watched him grow up. I never saw anything extraordinary come out of that carpenter's shop—a chair, here and there, of decent quality, but nothing of significance. Don't you believe a word of it." Not much of anything happened in that atmosphere. He came to his own, but they did not receive him.

John wrote that the promise was like light shining in the darkness and the darkness could not extinguish it. I have visited Mammoth Cave in Kentucky several times. During one tour, the guide stopped and turned out the lights. You've never seen dark until you have been deep in a cave surrounded by intense darkness void of any light. That is a blank that is ultimate darkness. But where there is light, the darkness vanishes. Light always dispels darkness, but darkness cannot dispel light. This is the message of promise.

Christianity is a religion of unquenchable faith and hope and patience; unquenchable because it believes that the permanent thing is light and the passing thing is darkness; that however long the night, whether in world affairs or the poignant, private world of the human heart, the night will pass. The permanence of the light is based on the promise of God. What is so overwhelming about the promise of God is that God's performance always exceeds God's promise. Perhaps you are familiar with the picture of an infant with the caption, "A child is God's affirmation that the world should continue." A children's song expresses a similar note. "I am a promise. I am a possibility with a capital P. I am a promise."

The light of promise has come. It has shined in the darkness and the darkness cannot put it out. The light of promise came to Abraham and Sarah and the darkness of Sarah's skepticism could not put it out. The promise of God lit the path of liberation for the Israelites. Neither Pharaoh's army nor the grumbling people could put it out. Centuries later, as the Israelites were captives in Babylonia, even the torture of exile could not destroy the promise. When the light of God's promise beamed in the eyes of Jesus, the pessimism of Nathaniel could not dim it.

The light of God's promise is brilliant and beaming. It cannot be put out. It can only be shut out. The promise of God does not protect us from debilitating disease, poverty, the ravages of war, or the pain of betrayal. The promise of God provides us with light so we can see our way through the darkness. The only guarantee we receive from the promise is that God will be our God, if we will be God's people. Strangely, as children of promise, that's the only guarantee we need.

PROPHETS OF MERCY

The role of the prophet has a long, significant history in biblical religion. The probable root meaning of the word is "to call" or "to announce." The prophet was a spokesperson. Abraham, Moses, Miriam, and Deborah were prophets in this sense, although they are not identified as prophets, while Jeremiah, Isaiah, Amos, and Hosea are.

The popular perception of prophecy is the ability to predict the future. Periodically, there is an increasing interest in predicting the future and many call it prophecy. There may be more emphasis on fortune telling, magic, and palm reading. I recently saw a sign that read, "Palm Reading at Discount Prices." The humor in that sign for me was that often in contemporary culture, prophecy is for profit. Our appetite for knowing the future is insatiable. Many are willing to pay unbelievable prices to know what they cannot know.

The biblical prophets took a different approach. They assessed their current situations and called attention to the logical consequences if life continued to be lived in that direction. The prophet whose words are recorded in the final chapters of Isaiah said that the Chosen People were chosen not to overwhelm the world in triumph, but to suffer and die for the world in love. No one has ever been comfortable with someone who made such suggestions.

Often, with no semblance of tact, biblical prophets roared out against phoniness and corruption wherever they found them. Political and religious leaders were their prime targets. They could ring terror in the hearts of kings and priests like no one else.

But being a prophet was not a job anyone wanted. There is no evidence that a biblical prophet ever applied for the job. Actually, the evidence is ample they went to great lengths to avoid and resist the job. Isaiah wanted to know how long his contract was to last. Jeremiah said he was too young. Moses said he was not any good at public speaking and he doubted if anybody would listen anyway. Most of the prophets bordered on insanity before they were finished, if they were not that way when they started. Ezekiel saw wheels with eyes around the rims. John the Baptist's main diet was bugs. Most of the prophets had an eccentric streak in them. Was it there before they began prophesying or did it develop with the job?

The prophet's quarrel with the world was like poet Robert Frost's—deep down it was a lover's quarrel. If the prophets had not loved the world they probably would not have bothered telling the world anything. They would have just let the world alone and let it go wherever its drift seemed to take it.

Here is a true story, a real-life drama. A young man from a fine family met a woman from the other side of the tracks. She was from a lower social class than he, but he was attracted to her. She had had few of the advantages that had been his. Her family's reputation was not good and there were some real questions about her morality. But the more this man saw this woman, the more he thought about her, and the more he wanted to be with her. He knew what his family would say about her and he knew how the people at church would treat her. Nevertheless, he decided to marry her and surround her with love, devotion, and security. He was just as right as rain—his family and the people at church said a lot of the things he had expected and even worse. But the couple's life together went well until some time after their first child was born. Then tension between them became more evident. The distance widened. The birth of the second child raised some suspicions about the woman's faithfulness, and with the birth of a third child the evidence seemed almost unmistakable that she had been unfaithful. Not long after the birth of the third child, the woman deserted her family and began living the life of a prostitute.

How do you react to the people and this situation? What are your feelings? What do you think about this man, woman, and their three children? I hope you would easily feel concern for the children. They had no control over their situation and did not contribute to the family's tragedy. Maybe you feel sorry for the husband or are angry with him. He had tried but he had been foolish to think a marriage could work with a woman whose family and background were so different than his. And what about the woman? She was given the chance of a lifetime to rise above her past and her roots, but she blew it. She did not take advantage of the great opportunity that was hers. And then to abandon her family, especially her children! What kind of woman was she? How ungrateful and irresponsible can she be!

What should the husband do? Get a divorce? Have absolutely nothing to do with this woman anymore? Reject the one who had rejected him? But what if he began to take steps to get her to come back? What if this man went so far as to pay her bail to get her out of jail? What if he continued to tell her he loved her, and he was willing to do anything he could to make a go of their marriage? He is crazier than we suspected, isn't he? What if this man began to put a religious spin on this life drama? What if he suggested that the way he felt toward his wife, his desire for them to make a go of their relationship, was the way God relates to people? Is this the final straw of sanity? Has the man really gone over the edge?

Well, this story happened in the eighth century B.C.E. Hosea is the man's name. He was a sensitive human being and a religious prophet. Although he must have spent some time in self-pity and thought about ways to get back at his wife, he did not allow his hostility to fester and consume him. He had an unquenchable love for Gomer. Rather than wanting to destroy Gomer, Hosea wanted her to see his love for her and join him in rebuilding their relationship. He even went to the slave auction and bought her in order to set her free. He paid a high price to show her his love and his dream that she be free. He was crushed but not destroyed. He kept on loving her and wanted her to love him.

Hosea was the first person to suggest that the way lovers are related to each other is the way God and people are related to each other. In the shambles of his marriage, Hosea began to see that the way Gomer had related to him was how Israel had related to God. This insight brought up for review Israel's history with God and resulted in Hosea experiencing deep in his own being the prophetic message he had heard proclaimed.

The prophets had pointed out that God had freed Israel from slavery, brought them to the Promised Land, they had gone back into slavery, and God was seeking them again. This was an often-repeated scenario. Hosea began to catch a glimpse of the source of his unquenchable love for Gomer. If he had such deep love for Gomer, then God's love for Israel was even deeper. What was the source of this deep love Hosea had for Gomer? His love for Gomer had roots in God's love for Israel. Hosea saw more clearly than anyone who had preceded him what sin really is and what God is truly like. Sin is the betrayal of the tender bond of love. Hosea found God's mercy to be everlasting.

I find all of this difficult to comprehend. My mercy is not as deep or broad as Hosea's. I would be one to tell Hosea he was a fool to have anything else to do with Gomer. Where is his sense of pride? Why would he let her walk all over him? But there God stands, refusing to tell me what a fool I am. There God stands, tears trickling down, arms open wide, seeking me, inviting me, welcoming me back into relationship.

This is what the light of prophecy is all about. This is what the first two chapters of Luke are all about. Biblical religion is brought to a climax in the life and ministry of Jesus.

Hosea and Jesus share a name in common, the Hebrew and Greek transliterations of the same name means "savior" or "salvation." But these two have more than their names in common. They also share a common identification with sorrow, suffering, anguish, and tragedy as a means for ministry. Both were spokespeople for God. Heartache and alienation accompanied both of them. Both walked through a valley of tears in loneliness and desolation, yet, through the valley found and pointed people toward the doorway of hope. The light of promise to which they bore witness was brightened by the light of the prophecy of mercy they spoke and lived.

The prophets tell us what God is like and what we can expect from God. Then, when we experience God coming to us, the awe and the warmth are always more than we expected or thought possible.

The birth of Jesus ought not be that surprising. God coming to dwell in people and with people was nothing new. God had been doing this from the foundation of the world. The everlasting mercy of God demonstrated so clearly in Jesus was nothing new. God's mercy had been there all along. Hosea discovered it and bore witness to it. Jesus lived out this kind of mercy as completely as any human being ever did or ever could. Here we are, twenty-one centuries later, being invited to discover and live out God's mercy in our time. One of the responses we can make to God is to be prophets of mercy.

But we argue against being such prophets. There are others better qualified. Others are more eloquent. Besides, we are so angered by the brutal acts of an individual or a group that we feel only raging terror or hatred for them. We want them destroyed. We do not want any mercy shown to them. The attitudes of Hosea and Jesus are foreign to us. If it is on the list at all, mercy is the last thing we are interested in feeling or expressing. We are not interested in loving unlovable people or being physicians to those who are sick. We certainly are not willing to show any mercy to those who have been unmerciful in their attitudes and actions.

Yet, we are recipients of this mercy. What about the times and circumstances in our lives when, through some prophet of mercy, God got through to us? We discovered we were being loved in spite of all the mess we had made. All of this was being done to bring us back into relationship with God.

If God has gone to such lengths for us, can we do less in our responses toward others? Jesus said to a loveless Pharisee one day, "I desire mercy, and not sacrifice" (Matt. 9:13 RSV). Learning how to receive mercy from God and learning how to give mercy fully and completely to others—this is the "Law and the Prophets."

Hosea only had two things to say when the light of this mercy began to shine in his life: "God is love," and "There is no end to it." This mercy became real for Hosea because it was localized in his relationship with Gomer. These words became flesh in Hosea and dwelt with people. These words became flesh in Jesus of Nazareth. The opportunity is before us for them to become flesh again, in you and me. If they do, once again Scripture will be fulfilled because new prophets of mercy will be born. What shall we be? Let's be prophets of mercy!

MAKERS OF PEACE

The likely progression is to become children of God's promise. Reflecting on the promise and the children we are and are becoming leads us to be prophets of mercy. If by word and deed we announce the mercy of God, we will experience ourselves becoming makers of peace. But it takes a long time for us to get the story right.

Kyle was a five-year-old boy whose favorite season of the year was Advent. His favorite passage of Scripture was, "Glory to God in the highest, peace on earth, goodwill to men." He was invited to be part of his church's Christmas pageant and he was going to get to say his favorite lines. The night of the pageant came. Kyle was excited. When it came time for him, Kyle entered the stage and there he was, in front of all those people with the lights pouring on him, and he began his lines, "Glory to God in the highest," but he couldn't remember the rest of it. He paused. His parents were in the audience pulling for him. Kyle tried again, "Glory to God in the highest . . . and I'll huff and I'll puff and I'll blow your house down." Kyle had gotten the story wrong.

We, too, have gotten the story wrong. We continue to perpetuate the wrong story. We can quote Jesus' words, "Happy are those who work for peace; God will call them his children!" But we have acted as though this were a comment we could take or leave rather than seeing it as an expectation of us if we follow him. The directive is emphasized in Paul's letter to the Romans: "Do everything possible on your part to live in peace with everybody." We certainly have gotten the story of peace wrong at this point.

Every religion has a strong clamor for peace. Woven throughout the Bible is both the desire and prescription for peace. Peace is the anchor of life. Our lives are solid, coherent, and congruent when we experience peace. Peace means completeness, wholeness, and health. Is there anyone who does not want life to be complete, rock solid, and whole, rather than fragmented, shattered, and disrupted? There are times when everything around us seems settled but our lives are shaky, and other occasions when the environment is exploding but our lives are calm and at peace.

God wants us to experience peace and completeness and wholeness. God offers and desires peace for us not as the world defines peace, but as a peace that keeps us from being worried and upset. We begin suffering from hardening of the emotions when we become anxious. We resist relationships, withdraw into our own cocoons, and become hard, crusty, and inhumane. But when we allow the presence of God to dwell with us, permeate our lives, and guide our relationships, we experience wholeness, completeness, and peace. We are pliable and our relationships are dynamic, expanding, inclusive, growing. We are at peace and our lives are anchored solidly in the peace of God that passes all understanding. It was this peace about which Micah prophesied. It was this peace that Micah challenged people to remember and to expect. It was this peace that came wrapped in swaddling clothes and lying in a manger two thousand years ago. This is the story of peace we are to remember and tell this day and every day.

The prophet Isaiah (11:1–9) imagined what peace would be like when the world receives the gift of peace from God. He suggests that the warring factions in nature will be reconciled to each other. The gift of God's peace changes things from the inside out so that their very nature and attitude are altered toward reconciliation. Isaiah had in mind a living king who would rule in such a distinct and different way from his predecessors that a whole new world order would be the result. The Israelites hailed every new king as the Lord's anointed who would usher in the golden age. A distinctive of this ruler, who would be a shoot of new growth, was that he would not make decisions based on appearances and accents. Because these new hopes were never realized under any of the kings, this description came to be the anticipation of one in the future who would be Messiah, the Anointed One of God. Generation after generation has found the description of God's peace in this passage.

It is Luke who has so much of nature involved in announcing the coming of God in human flesh, proclaiming "Peace on earth." Word and deed are inseparable in biblical thought. Promise and practice are flip sides of the same conviction. One does not exist without the other. To announce peace on earth by God was not only the giving of peace, but also the making and being of peace. As it turned out, the one who was born the Prince of Peace grew up to give peace. As he said later, "My peace I give to you; not as the world gives do I give to you" (Jn. 14:27 RSV).

The religion of the Bible portrays a God who is seeking to give peace to creation. Only in this religion do we have a God weeping for creation. The gods in other religions are portrayed as uninvolved and disinterested in what happens to their domains, or they are portrayed as wreaking havoc upon the world as the mood strikes them. But in biblical religion, the Son of God, the

Prince of Peace, the complete presence of God in human flesh, crests the hill overlooking Jerusalem and begins to sob, "O Jerusalem, Jerusalem, would that you knew the things that make for peace." Pastoral counselor James Dittes has said, "Ministry in the Christian sense often takes the form of grief work. I mean by that, it is having to live with the disappointment of wanting something for a people they do not want for themselves."[1] God always has been more committed to the goal of giving peace to people than we have. Jesus was neither giving up in despair nor blowing up in rage as he approached Jerusalem, but rather he was shedding real tears for its folly and fate. He had offered and continued to offer the gift of peace, but they could not, would not, receive his gift.

The need to experience peace as the anchor of life is prevalent for individuals and for nations. Because of our interrelatedness and interdependence with people throughout the universe, it behooves each of us to create peace in the corner of the world where we live, work, and play.

Yury Gagarin, Soviet cosmonaut and the first man in space, said, "Isn't our earth a spaceship hurtling through the expanses of the universe? That ship belongs to all of us, to all peoples, and its crew must live in peace and friendship."[2]

The creative handiwork of God underscores our precious stewardship as trustees of God's creation. Jesus in Gethsemane clearly suggested that if resisting evil with evil was the right approach, legions could be called in to do that (Mt. 26:53). But Jesus said the only way to redeem people is to demonstrate to them the love of God that will not let them go. This is a difficult journey, but it is the way Christ went and the path he invites any who follow him to take.

Our immediate reaction is fear. We have worshiped at the altars of force and might so long that we are frightened to do anything differently. Idols instill fear in us and make us fearful of doing anything differently. To do something differently might mean we would stop worshiping the idol, the false god, but it has its grip on us. Fear is the first line of disruption of peace. Our peace is broken when we give in to our fears and we begin disrupting the peace of others. Peace also is threatening, especially to those who are not at peace. Jealousy and envy have captured people, and they have wreaked havoc in people's lives who were at peace. These havoc wreakers conclude that they want other people to be at least as miserable as they are.

Many people fear the loud noise or catastrophe of a nuclear holocaust, if not caused by the super forces, then by a terrorist group. This fear can so overwhelm us at times that we are immobilized and suffer from what Harvard professor of psychiatry Robert Lifton calls "psychic numbing." We find ourselves caught in the crisis of basic trust versus basic mistrust. We are immobilized when the forces of trust and mistrust have mutual power. We feel this with the instability in the Middle East and the hopes of many that peace will break out there. Leaders and nations have difficulty finding space to maneuver when they box themselves in with charges and counter charges. Only as some psychic movement occurs can the conflict be resolved. The resolution gives birth to hope. With the birth of hope, we are able to name the fear of catastrophe and begin to experience peace in our lives and in our relationships that will lead to our seeking peace beyond ourselves and for others.

The tasting and testing of relationships begun during infancy continues throughout our lives in interactions with people we meet, groups we consider joining, and agreements made between nations. Agreements often are based on a mixture of trust and mistrust. There is a sense in which treaties made internationally between enemies are based on mistrust. Because there is mistrust of each other, there is a necessity to agree on some things as a means of being able to see each other eye-to-eye. Trust may evolve as the treaty is kept. The keeping of one agreement begins to establish the basis for hope that other agreements will be made and kept.

Mistrust leads to suspicion. Tension increases. Fear rises, and existence is threatened. People are motivated to violence because they suspect they have been betrayed and deceived. The development of trust depends greatly on the ability of infants to look into the eyes of their parents and vice versa. Eyes do serve as windows into people. We never outgrow our need to look into the eyes of others to establish trust and mutual recognition. We must get close enough to see people eye-to-eye. To look into people's eyes is to see the image of God indelibly marked in their lives. To see the image of God in others is to be creators of peace and to tell the story of peace.

One of the significant accomplishments of the summit meetings in recent years is that world leaders have seen each other eye-to-eye. While visiting the Soviet Union in 1983, a member of one of the Baptist churches commented to several of us, "Now that I see your faces, you are beautiful people." Here was an expression of the importance of looking into each other's eyes in order to establish trust. I am always glad when national leaders, especially those who have strong opposition to each other, agree to high-level talks. It is important for leaders of nations that have such strong, stringent differences to look at each other and talk face-to-face about the differences. Every possible avenue of peace must be sought.

The better we tell the story of peace, the better we prevent hardening of the emotions. There are at least four things we can do in our relationships with others at home, at church, at school, at work, wherever we are that will prevent hardening of the emotions and bring peace to others and to ourselves. First, we can develop the gift of affirmation. You may have heard the story of the little boy who woke up every morning with the image of this huge sign that read, "I am likeable and capable." He felt so good about himself, good to be alive, excited about the day. But his mother yelled at him for having such a messy room, for the clothes he chose to wear, and for wasting his time.

He still had his sign, but it was a bit smaller. At school, the teacher yelled at him because he couldn't read as well as she expected and he stumbled over the math problems. His sign got smaller. On the way home from school, a friend called him a dummy, and the sign got smaller. At dinner, his dad complained that all the boy ever wanted to do was play games, and the sign got smaller. When he went to bed, his parents were angry with him because he wanted them to read to him. His sign was so tiny that it was nearly nonexistent. This boy, who was likeable and capable, needed people who would affirm him and that would give him a sense of wholeness, peace, shalom.

How often do we give and receive verbal and nonverbal messages that say, "You're lazy!" "When are you going to do something worthwhile?" "What's the matter with you?" There is not a person anywhere who would not benefit from being affirmed. Before the creation of the world was completed, God paused, examined the creation, and pronounced, "It is very good." Who of us would not feel uplifted, at peace, if someone said, "I like you. You are important. I appreciate who you are. I like the gift of your smile. Your presence has been an encouragement to me"? How long has it been since you have said any of these things? Hardening of the emotions can be prevented when we feel respected and valued, when we feel we have been heard, and when we take time to listen to others.

A second prevention for hardening of the emotions is to have respect for people who are different than we are. Too often we summarize our ideas with a bumper sticker slogan and use verbal labels to categorize and stereotype people. Someone has said that if you can reduce what you think about an issue or situation to a bumper sticker statement, you haven't thought enough about the issue. We use labels to distance ourselves from others, often from those who seem very different from us. We enter into name-calling—names like Hippie, Peacenik, Freezenik, Chauvinist, Women's Libber, Nigger, Honkie, Arab, Jew, Liberal, Conservative! We equate a current world leader with Hitler or Stalin. Underneath such words is fear—fear of what being different from me is like. We need to discover one another's uniqueness, acknowledge each other's differences. To discover the uniqueness of a person requires involvement and interaction with others, a willingness to risk being known, at least slightly, and being open, ever so slightly, to the possibility of changing our minds.

The challenge of cooperation rather than the glory of competition is a third way to prevent hardening of the emotions. Competition divides people into winners and losers. This happens to individuals and between nations. Much of the distance between the Soviet Union and the United States over the years was an unwillingness to discuss and work cooperatively. Thus, the emotions between the two nations hardened. Cooperation through summit meetings softened international emotions toward each other and made the relationship more pliable and workable. The cooperation between nations recently has been remarkable and unprecedented. We are entering a new world era in which nations must see and relate to each other as one among equals rather than clamoring for the selfish status of number one. We can develop a cooperative attitude in our personal relationships that will contribute to an atmosphere of trust and acceptance that lessens the we-they mentality fostered in a competitive environment.

A fourth step in preventing hardening of the emotions is to seek creative and constructive resolutions to conflict. To be alive is to experience conflict.

Part of the paradox of the Prince of Peace and his efforts to give peace was that trouble followed him wherever he went. The gift of peace was so radical, so much at the root of life, that for many people, to receive this gift uprooted so much of their lives that they held on all the more tenaciously. The gift of peace that Christ modeled and offered involved reconciliation between people and God. Such reconciliation requires a switching of loyalties. A certain amount of turmoil, naturally, is involved when some loyalties are thawing and others are being formed. Jesus accurately described this process of bringing a sword rather than peace. Even the surgeon's scalpel that brings healing and wholeness does so only by causing pain and hurt before the peace of health comes. Most who undergo surgery feel worse for a while after surgery than prior to it. The gift of peace Christ offers often makes us feel worse before it helps us feel better, because it involves a switching of loyalties, which involves instability and insecurity as change occurs.

Too often we claim that peace is the absence of conflict. There will be conflict with people in and out of the church. There will be conflict in our families. There will be conflict at school, at work, between nations. Conflict will exist. The question is how will it be resolved. Inevitably, there will be conflict wherever there is a relationship because two people will have different needs that arise simultaneously. The philosopher Spinoza said, "Peace is not an absence of war; it is a virtue, a state of mind, a disposition for benevolence, confidence, justice." Peace is the result of a creative resolution of conflict so that the relationship is enhanced and harmony between the parties is increased.

To ignore conflict or to refuse to seek conflict resolution results in hardening of emotions. Affirmation of others, acceptance of the differences of others, and a cooperative spirit all contribute to making emotions pliable and lead to constructive resolutions of conflict.

We have a story to tell. It is the story of peace. Like Kyle, we often have gotten the story wrong. Now more than ever, we need to get the story right. The peace story is best told and best understood when it is our life's story. Those who create peace are called the children of God. We are called to a ministry of reconciliation, which means that at home, at school, at work, at church, on the highway, and at the ball game, we are to create a climate for peace, an attitude, a frame of mind of well-being for others, wholeness, and completeness.

We tell best the story that we are in the process of hearing and learning ourselves. We will experience peace, calmness, and centeredness that will cause our lives to feel whole as we encounter and experience resolutions to the conflicts that rage in our lives. Then our living becomes the storytelling of peace. As we tell the story of peace we become makers of peace, and we are, in fact, the children of God.

CONDUCTORS OF LOVE

Peggy Lee sang the song, but all of us have asked the question, "Is that all there is?" Never more often is this our question than during the Christmas season. The question is not an expression of greed that we want more gifts. Rather, the question is a way we acknowledge that we have a longing, a hunger, a desire that cannot be filled with food or tinsel wrapped packages. There really is more to life, more to Christmas than this. We feel a kinship with Charlie Brown.

Here is what happened in one episode of the "Peanuts" comic strip. Lucy has a score to settle with Charlie Brown. She chases him, shouting, "I'll get you, Charlie Brown! I'll get you. I'll knock your block off!"

Charlie Brown, who has been running full speed, stops, turns around and says, "Wait a minute! Hold everything! We can't carry on like this! We have no right to act this way. . . . The world is filled with problems. . . . People hurting other people. . . . People not understanding other people. . . . Now, if we as children can't solve what are relatively minor problems, how can we ever expect to . . . "

Lucy then interrupts Charlie Brown in mid-sentence, hitting him with a left to the jaw, knocking him out. Says Lucy, "I had to hit him QUICK! He was beginning to make sense!"

Have you ever wished that some of the kindness, togetherness, and love that are shown occasionally would be shared throughout life? Would it not be great if we could go through a month squeezing out all the frantic activity and saving everything that makes us feel warm, loved, accepted, the things that move us to tears and crack our faces with smiles?

What we need is people who will help us feel welcome in life. What we need is to help others feel welcome in life. Have you ever felt unwelcome somewhere? There are few experiences in life more painful than to be unwelcome. A pastor in South Carolina told of being at a state correctional institution and watching, day after day, fathers come to visit their imprisoned sons. He watched them as they applied at the front office and then as they waited for their sons to be called down to the visitors' room. Time and again, many of these fathers would be disappointed. The prison guard would return with the news, "Sorry, sir, your son says that he doesn't want to see you."

The father would gather his packages and walk out the front door of the prison. But the next week, on the next visiting day, the father would be back.

"Even if he were sent away for a hundred days, he would always come back the next week and ask to visit his son," the pastor said.

God is like that. Even when we reject God's love, as we have done so often and so thoughtlessly, God continues to come back year after year, because God loves us. The Advent and Christmas season is a time when we focus on God coming to dwell with us, welcoming us to the world, and desiring to be welcomed into our lives.

Hospitality is one of the essential ingredients of the season and spirit of Christmas. Basic to this season is to welcome and be welcomed by God. We do that by welcoming people into our lives and permitting others to welcome us into theirs. This calls for us to reexamine the meaning of serving and servanthood. The world's view and the biblical view of serving and the servant are diametrically opposed to each other. The world's view is one of being served. Importance, status, and prestige come with being served, according to the popular view. Being on top of the pyramid with everyone beneath serving the one on top is the world's image of serving. But the biblical image of serving is that of an inverted pyramid where the truly great people are depicted as those who serve others.

I imagine each of us knows someone who is just natural as a gracious host or hostess. You feel like a guest whenever you are in this person's presence. You are at ease and have no concern about any needs because you sense, without even thinking about it, that you are being taken care of.

Hospitality is basic to servanthood. It means to be liberal and generous in disposition and mind. To be hospitable is to be receptive and open to people and their ideas. It is a virtue that enables us to break through the narrowness of our own fears and to open our lives to strangers.

Two things are required for hospitality: concentration and community. A person becomes our guest when she walks into our lives. We must pay attention to her and not be preoccupied with our needs. We struggle to pay attention to another because of our intentions. When our intentions take over, we ask, "What can I get from her?" rather than, "What does she need?" When our intentions are ruling, we no longer listen to what another is saying, but we seek to determine what we can do with what she is saying. Hospitality requires concentration so that we focus on meeting the needs of the strangers who have come into our lives.

Community also is necessary for hospitality. Although we often attempt to be Lone Rangers, we are made so that relating to others really is an essential, necessary characteristic of being human. The earliest stories of the creation of human beings say, "It is not good for a person to be alone."

In his book *Fundamentals of Preaching*, John Killinger tells of the days when news of the old country was carried to America only by ships. People would assemble at the dock when a mast was sighted:

The moment a gangplank was thrown up and sailors began to disembark, hands would stretch out and cries would go up from the crowd beseeching, "Is there any word?" And I can testify, as one who has often gone to church with the masses of modern men and women who feel isolated, cut off from community, lost in the wasteland of electronics and gadgetry that we enter the sanctuary with the same plea: "Is there any word?"[3]

When we are hospitable people, we provide a friendly space where people are free to come and go. We can offer them a word. The word is love. God loves us. The more we believe that, the more love will dominate the way we relate to others. In this way, we become hospitable people who bring healing by giving ourselves in serving others because it is the loving, godly thing to do.

Christmas is about hospitality. God is the great and grand host who seeks to care for and serve the world by paying attention to our needs, enabling us to feel comfortable in God's presence, and helping us establish a community in and through which we relate to God and fellow human beings. To see and experience Christmas in this light calls for us to develop an alternative view of the meaning and practice of being a servant to others. Being a servant ceases to be a menial task and becomes the crowning expression of love, grace, and acceptance. The Son of God came into the world not to be served, but to serve. We who are created in the image of God are called to be the children of God and are also in the world not to be served, but to serve. This whole approach turns the world's view of service and servanthood on its ear. It really turns the world's view of serving upside down, which actually is right side up. All of this calls for us to welcome people into our presence, into our lives, to be an outstanding host or hostess to those who are guests in our lives.

I spent some time on the farm with my grandparents almost every summer of my childhood. I enjoyed learning to do things on the farm and becoming an able helper and worker with my grandfather. I still recall the shock I caused during one of my attempts to be helpful. My grandfather had constructed an electric fence around part of a pasture area for his cattle. It was important to test the fence periodically to be certain it was working. Early one morning, as he and I were walking on that part of the farm, I took a large blade of grass and touched it to the electric fence. I felt no electrical sensation. I tapped the wire, still no shock. I grasped the wire with my hand. No shock. The electric fence wasn't working. I had done a good thing making this discovery. I told my grandfather the fence wasn't working and held the wire with my hand to show him. He grasped the wire and got the shock of his life! He looked me over sternly. Both of us were standing in tall, wet fescue, but I was wearing rubber overshoes, and he was not. I was grounded! The electrical impulse could not pass through me to the ground.

In order to be conductors of love, we must receive God's love, but not just for ourselves. We permit the love of God to flow to us and then through us to others. To receive God's love for ourselves, but not permit it to flow through us to others is to stop the flow of God's love to ourselves as well as to others. We will be unable to sense God's love even though it is there. Without sensing it, we cannot benefit from it, and it cannot benefit others. A baby was left on the doorstep many years ago of a home in Georgetown, Pennsylvania. A widow was the head of that home—a widow with several children to look after. But she took in that baby and loved it like her own. She would read great books to her children in the evenings, and one of them, at least, developed a great taste for literature. That baby abandoned on a doorstep was one of America's most prolific writers, James Michener.

James Michener's life was a triumph of the unselfish love of that widowed mother. That is the kind of love we celebrate this season—love for one another. It is this kind of hospitality we are to offer to the world. It has been offered to us and we have gladly received it. We are to share what we have received. What we do not share, we lose.

Of course, we do not completely comprehend how all of this works in our lives. It really makes no sense to us that God, who created the universe, who had such power and ability, would be interested in each of us individually. How does God have that kind of time and energy?

Perhaps, in cosmic terms, the earth is a tiny planet. But it is the planet to which God sent His Son! We are a God-visited planet, to use novelist C. S. Lewis's words. God has paid us the ultimate compliment of being present to us in our world.

We approach our understanding of the meaning and purpose of Christmas like the pastor who served Communion to children. This pastor, who was leading a discussion in a seminary class, was asked by one of the students, "Do you serve the children Holy Communion?"

"Most definitely," he replied.

"But do you think children are old enough to understand its meaning?"

"What meaning?" the pastor asked. The student appeared thoughtful and the pastor pressed the question. "What is it about Holy Communion that you understand that the child is unable to understand?" More silence followed, and it seemed the entire class was paralyzed.

After a few moments, the pastor went on, "We belong to Christ. Christ receives us. For Christ to say, 'Take, this is my body,' is for Christ to say, 'Take me, I'm yours.' It is Christ's way of receiving us."

Children may not know how to express Christ's receiving them in intellectual terms, but children know what it means to feel included. We should never deny them participation in a birthday dinner because they cannot explain its meaning. We do not deny them the experience of Christmas because they cannot comprehend the meaning of incarnation. Why, then, should we deny them Holy Communion? If we truly believe that Christ's receptivity embraces even the children, why deny them a seat at the Lord's Table? Although it is true that they cannot explain things with intellectual sophistication, they know what it means to belong, to feel welcome, and they

WHAT SHALL WE BE?

know how much it hurts to feel excluded.[4]

Often it is children who make observations about life that are clear and concise. What they say often is what we feel and would like to say, but have become too inhibited by what others might think of us. Or we just don't see the point or the value of something, but will never admit it for fear someone will think we are dumb.

When one little boy was told about his new baby sister, he was not impressed. When he went to school the following day, his teacher remarked, "I hear you have a new member of your family."

"Oh, yeah," he replied.

"What's the matter?" his teacher asked. "Aren't you happy to have a new sister?"

He answered, "Yes, I guess. But there were a lot of things we needed more."

I am certain that when people hear the Christmas story for the first time, their initial reaction is that what the world needs most is not another baby. How wrong they are! Someone has said that when God wants something done in this world he has a baby born. We know that was true of the birth of Jesus of Nazareth. The prophet had spoken of old, "Behold a young woman shall conceive and bear a son, and shall call his name Immanuel" (Isa. 7:14 RSV). The Messiah has been born to Mary and Joseph in the little town of Bethlehem.

It was in a stable that he was born. What a strange place for the nativity of the King of Kings. What plain and shabby surroundings for the birth of the Messiah. I read sometime back about a South African diamond miner who found one of the world's largest diamonds. It was the size of a small lemon. The miner needed to get the diamond safely to the company's office in London, so he sent it in a small steel box and hired four men to carry it. Even when it was in the ship's safe en route, it was guarded day and night by at least two armed men. But when the package arrived at the company's office in London and was carefully opened, it contained no diamond. Rather, it contained a lump of black coal. Three days later, the diamond arrived by ordinary parcel post in a plain package. The owner had assumed correctly that most people would not pay attention to an ordinary cardboard box.

How often do the most precious things in life come in the most ordinary packages? Just consider for a moment the most important thing that has ever happened to you in your life. What is it? Do you have it clearly in mind? Now think about how that event happened to you. Did it come with fanfare and ticker tape parade? Or did it sneak in on cats' paws?

A manger and a stable are not much to begin with either. And yet, when a tiny babe was born in those humble surroundings, the greatest peace movement the world has ever known was born as well. That's how God accomplishes things. We are called to receive God's love in our lives and to live lives of love relating and caring for others as we have experienced God caring for us. We are to do what we can to be good hosts and hostesses, to serve others and thus to be of help to them as others have cared for and helped us.

Many years ago, there was a terrible earthquake in Alaska. Anchorage was devastated. A number of people wrote to the governor and demanded that he do certain things for them. They outlined the suffering that they had endured and demanded that the state take responsibility. Later the governor appeared on television and reported that, among all the demands, he had received a letter from a boy who had written on a 3 x 5 card and had taped to it two nickels. The boy had written these words: "Use this wherever it is needed. If you need more, let me know."

The clearest and most important message about God in the Bible is the promise and assurance that God will be with us at all times, in all circumstances, caring for us. We matter to God. Pastor Martin Niemoeller affirmed this truth in Dachau prison on Christmas Day, 1944. You may recall that he was imprisoned by Hitler because of his continuing declaration of the Christian faith in the face of demands that he tone it down. On this day, he was permitted to hold services for some of the prisoners. Few of them were to emerge alive from their imprisonment; many of them had been and would be tortured by their captors. What does a Christian minister say in a situation like that? Niemoeller preached on the text, "And his name shall be called Emmanuel, which means 'God is with us.'" He pointed out that they were not alone in their days of suffering and imprisonment. God was with them, even there, to save them from their sins, to comfort and strengthen them in persecution, to give them courage in the face of torture, and to keep their hope alive. They could be certain about this, he said, because in Jesus Christ, God is with us.

There is an old story about a skeptic, who, on meeting the local priest, greeted him as follows: "Hello, Father. Tell me this. What is the difference between Christ's mother and my mother?" "I don't know, Doctor," replied the priest, "but there is a very great difference between the sons."

There may be a great deal of difference between Mary's son and you and me, but we need to work to reduce the difference. Like Mary's son, you and I need to become conductors of love. The only view and vision of God that many people will ever have is what they see in you and me. That's why we need to be more diligent in our desire to serve others, to be people of hospitality. Our tendency is to try a little kindness for a week or two.

The College of William and Mary is located in Williamsburg, Virginia, named for King William and Queen Mary who established the school in 1691. It is the second oldest college in the United States and the first college established in the South. It has a great tradition. Many forward steps were taken in education within those hallowed walls. The first Phi Beta Kappa chapter, the honorary scholastic fraternity esteemed throughout the academic world, was organized there. It was there the honor system was established.

They pioneered this idea of students policing themselves against cheating, lying, and stealing. It was there the lecture system was first developed for teaching and training in the fields of medicine and law and other areas.

In the Reconstruction period years following the U. S. Civil War, the South lay devastated—the houses and farms were destroyed—the economy was wrecked. The College of William and Mary suffered greatly. There came a day when there was no money to rebuild. There were no students. There were no resources and it looked as though there was no interest whatsoever in continuing this kind of education. So, in 1881, the school was closed. Weeds grew on the campus, the roof tumbled in, the window lights were broken, and it was abandoned, forgotten, a lost cause save for the efforts of one man.

President Benjamin S. Ewell determined that the cause he loved and to which he had given his life—the founding of a school to perpetuate the liberal arts and the training of young men for the pulpit and to perpetuate the Christian faith—that cause would not die. So, without a budget, with only a deserted campus in ruins, President Ewell went every morning to the tower and rang the bells calling the school to classes. He acted as though the school was still there and kept the dream alive. People thought he was crazy. He was certainly foolish, for the cause was lost. But, for seven years—every day—President Ewell rang the bells at William and Mary in defiance of the despair and hopelessness that would destroy everything that he held valuable. As a result, the dream did not die. Today, William and Mary is a thriving school with a high academic standing because one man kept ringing the bell.

That is our mission, is it not? To keep ringing the bells of Christmas—to tell the world that Jesus Christ has come into our world. The most convincing way to do it is by serving other people by loving and caring for them, being compassionate toward them, and helping to form community with them so they will have space and a place to be themselves, affirming their need to relate to fellow human beings, discovering in those relationships the presence, care, love, and grace of God. Ring the bells of God's love for the world, God's love for you and me. Ring the bells of Christmas by loving and serving the world for God's sake. What shall we be? Let's be conductors of love.

QUESTIONS TO PONDER

1. Which of these is it easier for you to be: child of promise, prophet of mercy, maker of peace, or conductor of love? Why?

2. Which of these is it most difficult for you to be: child of promise, prophet of mercy, maker of peace, or conductor of love? Why?

3. What does it mean to you for God to guarantee you a relationship, but not guarantee you protection?

4. What actions could you take and statements could you make that would be prophetic in the sense that Hosea was prophetic?

5. What is the most important thing that has ever happened to you? How did it happen? When did you know it was the most important thing to have happened to you? How is God coming to you and dwelling in you like that experience?

6

WHAT THE WORLD NEEDS

1 TIMOTHY 6:11–21

Communication and travel technology shrink the world a little every day. We can instantly communicate with any place on the globe. The reduction in communication barriers, however, has not reduced the tensions in the world. Actually, we feel greater tension, and the possibility of the tension erupting into permanent division and destruction is a great possibility.

There are many things that divide the world: ideologies, economics, politics, and culture. The world's divisions are evident in numerous places: conservatism and liberalism, the haves and the have-nots, socialism and democracy, established countries and developing nations. We live in a divided world. People who claim to worship the same God and serve the same Christ have been responsible for a large portion of the division in the world. Too often we have attempted to get a corner on the truth and then sought to hold the truth captive, demanding that others view life like we do and perceive being disciples of Christ like we perceive it.

FAITH

The need has never been greater for faith to be elevated to an authentic expression of people's relationship with God, for justice to roll down like a never-ending stream, for kindness to be shown at every level of relationships, and for truth to be spoken in love. Truly, what the world needs now is faith, justice, love, and truth.

While the world gets smaller because of technology, our neighborhood needs to get larger because of the same technology. Our neighbors are the people who live next door to us and the people who live just on the other side of the world from us. Our neighbors are anybody and everybody, but nothing is real until it is local. We love God and we love our neighbors when we put our talking heads and our flailing arms together and hug the people around us by accepting and loving them for who they are, people that God created, our brothers and sisters in community, the community of God. Then we can sing in truth the truth of the song "We are one in the bond of love, we have joined our spirit with the spirit of God. We are one in the bond of love." The words of Edwin Markham's poem, "Outwitted," express well what needs to take place through love:

> He drew a circle that shut me out-
> Hectic, rebel, a thing to flout.
> But Love and I had the wit to win:
> We drew a circle that took him! [1]

One of the results of this bond of love is that it affects our eyes. Our ability to see is greatly improved by the bond of the love of God. We begin to see people where we once saw objects or problems or barriers or division. We begin to see the world, or at least part of it, like God sees it. With our new vision, we are able to see that what the world needs is faith, justice, kindness, and truth. Only as we begin to vision what the world needs will we begin to live these needs. Living these needs is incarnating them.

Methodist minister Mark Trotter told the story of a country boy who was invited to a fancy dinner. Surrounding him at the table were well-mannered aristocrats. In the course of the meal, he got a large, hot piece of potato in his mouth. He spit it out in the palm of his hand and put it on his plate. The genteel company was shocked. They cleared their throats and diverted their eyes, but he looked right at them and said, "You know a fool would have swallowed that." Religious faith is not a matter of swallowing a lot of beliefs.[2]

Perhaps more than anyone in recent years, James Fowler, professor at Emory University, has helped us to understand faith and the ways that faith develops:

> Faith . . . is a universal human concern. Prior to our being religious or irreligious, before we come to think of ourselves as Catholics, Protestants, Jews, or Muslims, we are already engaged in issues of faith. Whether we become nonbelievers, agnostics, or atheists, we are concerned with how to put our lives together and with what will make life worth living. Moreover, we look for something to love that loves us, something to value that gives us value, and something to honor and respect that has the power to sustain our being.[3]

> Faith is not a religious belief or doctrine, but the values about which one is ultimately concerned which cause one to act or to resist. These are the nonnegotiables of a person's life. Faith expresses our search for meaning in life and shapes the way we invest our deepest loves and our most costly loyalties. The people, causes, and institutions we really love and trust form the pattern of faith we live, the images we have of good and evil, of possibility and probability to which we are committed.[4]

Faith in contrast to belief has been expressed well by Wilfred Cantrell Smith, professor at Harvard:

> Faith is deeper, richer, and more personal. It is engendered by a religious tradition, in some cases and to some degree by its doctrines; but it is a quality of the person not of the system. It is an orientation of the personality, to oneself, to one's neighbor, to the universe; a total response; a way of seeing whatever one sees and of handling whatever one handles; a capacity to live at more than a mundane level; to see, to act in terms of, a transcendent dimension.[5]

Faith is a quality of living. It is a means of being at home in the universe. As a result, one faces and deals with life with a quiet confidence and joy. Life takes the form of serenity and courage and loyalty and service. One finds meaning in life that is profound and ultimate and is stable no matter what may happen in an immediate event. People of this kind of faith face catastrophe and confusion, affluence and sorrow, unperturbed. They face opportunity with conviction and drive and face others with cheerful charity.

Blaise Pascal, French mathematician, scientist, and philosopher, was at work in his laboratory soon after the death of his beloved daughter when a scientist friend stopped by to see him. Observing Pascal's faith and quiet trust in the face of his tragedy, the friend said, "Pascal, I wish I had your creed, then I would live your life." Pascal replied calmly, but firmly, "Live my life and you will soon have my creed."

Clarence Jordan, founder of Koinonia Farms in Americus, Georgia, noted that faith is not a stubborn belief in spite of all evidence. That is not faith, that is foolishness. Faith is not belief in spite of evidence, but a life in scorn of the consequences.[6]

Near the end of his life, the apostle Paul wrote to Timothy, "I have done what was necessary in my time; now you must do what is necessary in your time." Paul used the athletic scene as a metaphor for the faithful response of a disciple of Christ. One can imagine the marathon in the background as Paul wrote, "I have fought the good fight, I have finished the race, I have kept the faith" (2 Tim. 4:7 NRSV). Theologian and writer Thomas Oden summarizes what Paul wrote this way, "I have not dodged the responsibility given me. I have not gone about it halfheartedly. I have been given a race to run. I gave it my all."[7] The energy of this metaphor is fixed upon finishing, not on winning, triumphing, or being crowned. It is a major accomplishment just to finish a marathon. Paul is not praising himself, but giving thanks to God for the grace to finish the race, for the joy of having been enabled to endure the whole contest.

We are asked, invited, called to be faithful to God in the marathon of life. We identify ourselves as disciples. Like the disciples we read about in the Gospels, God called us through our understanding of Christ to be disciples, learners who share God's love with others. This calling is an invitation to promise to live our lives in ways that communicate God's love and care for the world. By making such a promise, we are responding with our love and loyalty that finds expressions in many ways and through a variety of avenues.

We belong to a community of faith. That community may be a congregation with a name or it may be what Baptist pastor Carlyle Marney identified as our own private church. Marney identified those few, intimate friends in our lives who know us best and love us most unconditionally as our authentic church, community of faith. We are ourselves with these people, warts and all. Our love and loyalty to God is demonstrated through these relationships. This calls for faithfulness.

It calls for faithfulness in worship. Whether private or public, worship is rehearsal. It is where we practice how we are to live. Then, we go from worship and live. We do some things well, and some we don't do so well. We return to worship to practice again.

Practice is a significant discipline of any sports team. My high school basketball coach made the games fun for us, partly because practice was so difficult. The games really were easier physically. On occasion, a better team won the game, but we were never defeated because a team was better prepared or in better condition than we were. Part of my weekly routine several years ago was to observe practice by several sports teams at Auburn University. I noticed a similar attitude by all the coaches. They conducted serious, hardworking practices with certain objectives to accomplish in practice. I observed that, in many ways, the games or meets were easier than practice. I also noticed that people who did not practice and who did not really put themselves into practice did not play and were not put into game situations.

Here is one of my favorite stories. A young boy was carrying his violin in its case walking on the sidewalk in downtown Philadelphia. He stopped a man he was meeting and said, "Excuse me, sir. Could you tell me how to get to Carnegie Hall?" The man responded, "Practice, my boy, practice." We could say to God, "Excuse me, God, but could you tell me how to know what to do and how to live each day?" And God responds, "Worship, my people, worship." We are called to be faithful in worship because worship is our practice for how we are to live.

We are called to be faithful in study. Study also is both private and public. Reading, meditating, and studying scripture are valuable and essential for our spiritual growth and development. There is great merit in studying scripture, reading insights that others have on passages, and reflecting on what you have read. But our study must not stop with our own private reflection. The result will be too narrow of an understanding, too few insights into a passage, and too few applications of what we have read. We benefit from engaging others in conversations about what we have read, studied, or thought.

We need to find the best resources and tools available to help us explore, understand, and examine the Bible. We need to know about the context as well as the content of what we read. We need to find ways to translate the written word of God into the living word of God through the incarnation of God's word into our lives. Some people's lives are the best sermons you'll ever hear. We are called to be faithful in our study.

We are called to be faithful in our stewardship. Created in the image of God, God has asked us to manage our lives, to be good stewards of them because we have been asked to look after what God has given us. We are called to be faithful stewards of our lives. We need to be good managers of our minds, bodies, spirits, and the resources of the world that are at our disposal.

We are called to be faithful in our care and nurture of one another. In the book *The Color Purple*, two women are in conversation about church and God: "She say, Celie, tell the truth, have you ever found God in church? I never did. I just found a bunch of folks hoping for him to show. Any God I ever felt in church I brought in with me. And I think all the other folks did too. They come to church to share God, not find God."[8] When we are faithful in our nurture and care of others, we help each other share God. Nobody ever finds God. If there is any finding, it is God finding us rather than we finding God.

There is no way any of us can know and relate closely and intimately with every person we know. We can have an intimate relationship with a relatively few people, perhaps a maximum of ten to twelve people. What would happen if you sought each month to get to know one person better? Within a year, you would know twelve people better. I wonder what that would do for a spirit of support and encouragement within your family or where you work. I wonder what effect that would have on people in the community where you live. I wonder. Truly, the world needs people who relate better to each other.

We are called to be faithful in our conversations with and about each other. What is your first inclination when you hear a rumor? The first inclination of many is to tell the rumor to another person. To be faithful in our conversations, when we hear a rumor, we need to go to the person and find out if what we have heard is rumor or fact. Chances are what we have heard will be a blend of fact and fiction. We have little control over what others say. We can have all kinds of influence on what we say to and about others.

When was the last time you spoke a positive word about one person to another person? If you find yourself often making negative comments about another person or your employer, maybe it's time for an AA meeting—an Attitude Adjustment meeting. Maybe it is time for you to ask what is the source of this negative attitude you have and what can be done about it. Being a naysayer does not enrich the individual nor the group or organizations to which that individual belongs. Being faithful in our conversations builds up, rather than tears down. Truly, the world needs some building.

We are called to be faithful in our inclusion of others. No one is outside the realm of acceptability. Never in history has so much diversity been so evident as what we see and experience at the opening of the twenty-first century. To be inclusive creates difficulty and tension. Some people will be uncomfortable with such openness. There are those who feel a lot more secure with sameness rather than diversity. But the body of Christ is made up of many members. As part of the body of Christ, we are called to be inclusive. Let's enjoy and celebrate our diversity. Jesus related in a way to love everybody. We are invited to do the same.

To love everybody and to invite and welcome anybody and everybody into relationship is a liberal idea. If you don't believe that, just try this week to show love to every person you meet and invite someone very different from you into conversation and possible friendship with you. Think of people you know who have been shut out of relationships and start loving and caring for them. You'll discover what a liberal idea that is and what resistance and harassment such an attitude and actions cause. We are called to be faithful in our inclusion of others.

As one person has observed, there are two ways to get a chicken out of an egg. One way is with a hammer, but something of the chicken is lost in the process. A better way is for the mother hen to sit patiently on the egg, surrounding it with warmth, until it is time to hatch. There are two ways to command faith, one is by hammering us over the head; the other is with warming our hearts with love. God has chosen the second, less spectacular, way.

Donald Miller, professor at the University of Southern California, discovered value in searching and seeking that eventually led him back to a congregation. Miller looked at alternative meaning systems. He tried nothing for a while and then tried therapy. He returned to a congregation because it provided a tradition in which he could locate himself.

Miller's experience underscores British author G. K. Chesterton's observation, "When people stop believing in God, they do not believe in nothing. They believe in anything."[9]

A euphemism used by some people, regarding those who get excited about their faith, is that they are "on fire for God." Some even use such a statement to suggest that if a person doesn't have that kind of enthusiasm, their faith is in question. Such an attitude implies that if your faith is exciting, life will be comfortable, fun, exciting, delightful. Well, we really need to read our Bibles more closely. Here are several examples. Abel caught fire and Cain killed him. Abraham caught fire and found himself sacrificing Isaac. Sarah caught fire and spent her ninetieth birthday in the maternity ward. Rachel caught fire and died in childbirth. Joseph caught fire and was sold by his brothers into slavery. The Hebrews caught fire and wandered forty years in the wilderness. Moses caught fire and spent the rest of his life listening to the complaints and whining of a "stiff-necked" people. Deborah caught fire and had to lead an army. Naomi caught fire and was dealt with "bitterly." David caught fire and Solomon got to build the Temple. Job caught fire and lost his fortune and family. Daniel caught fire and was cast into the lion's den. Elijah caught fire and sat down dejectedly under a juniper tree to die. Jeremiah caught fire and felt "the arrows of God's quiver to enter into my veins." Hosea caught fire and married a prostitute. Elizabeth caught fire and her only son was beheaded. Stephen caught fire and was stoned. Paul caught fire and was shipwrecked and imprisoned. Mary caught fire and ended up an unmarried mother. Jesus caught fire and was beaten and crucified.

The fire of faith may begin to burn in your life. And you will sense a call to be faithful to God. The response to that call takes the shape of expressions of love. Those expressions do not always result in comfortable, popular experiences, but that is no reason to reject the call to faithfulness. Nor is it a reason to avoid responding in love.

We are called to be faithful to God. Being faithful to God leads to many responses. We respond by worshiping God. We respond by engaging in study, meditation, and reflection. We respond by being good managers and stewards of our lives. We respond by caring for and nurturing relationships with others, enlarging our circle of relationships. We respond by drawing ever-larger circles of inclusion. We respond in love by caring for and loving everybody. We are called to be faithful. May we continue to respond by finding ways to love the world for God's sake. May it be said of us, "They fought a good fight, they finished the course, they gave the faith away." What the world needs now is faith, faith incarnate—seen and known in the flesh of human beings.

PEACE

What the world needs now is faith because faith leads to peace. We need light for our lives and the more light the better. The brightest and best light for living is the light that peace offers. We are congruent when peace shines in our lives. To use a popular phrase, "we've got it together." We experience a calmness within which no raging storm from without can shatter.

Several years ago, Hurricane Andrew blew ashore at Homestead, Florida. I wondered about the hundreds of thousands of people in southern Florida whose lives were being turned upside down, threatened, and maybe destroyed, while I enjoyed a beautiful, sun drenched, amazingly cool August morning, my first day back to work following vacation. Compared with what was happening to people in southern Florida, life was astonishingly peaceful for me.

As I heard interviews with people who were working in shelters in the path of the storm, I was intrigued by how calm they were. How could they be so at ease knowing that a devastating, life-threatening storm was raging just miles away and headed straight for them?

I hope none of us will ever have to endure a storm like Hurricane Andrew. Yet, there are devastating storms that crash through our lives. Some of them provide us with advance warnings like the weather service was able to provide for people in Florida. Other storms occur suddenly, without warning. How can we not only survive such storms, but also live with meaning in the midst of, during, and after the onslaught of the havoc, bedlam, and chaos that accompany these storms?

An old Chinese proverb says, "Go to the heart of trouble and there you will find peace." Indeed, there is an astounding, unbelievable calmness in the eye or center of a hurricane. Often, in the midst of a raging storm in our lives, we experience a peace that surprises and astonishes us. Why is that? What is the source of that peace? Is there any way to develop peace like that so it is a part of our lives all the time?

The Advent season says the answer is yes. The Advent season says that by responding positively to God, who is asking to dwell in our lives, the light of peace will shine in our lives and provide light all around us to enhance our vision.

The world has changed dramatically in recent years. The tensions between the East and West have been greatly reduced, but conflict, hostility, and chaos have arisen in other places. People seem unwilling to get along. People starve in a nation while those in power make money by selling the food that is intended to go to those who are starving. What kind of humane action is this? How can those people live in peace? If they are not living in peace, then neither are we because, as John Donne wrote, "No man is an island, entire of himself."

St. Mary of Bethlehem Hospital was established in 1247 in England. However, about two hundred years later, it became a facility for the mentally ill. St. Mary of Bethlehem became a place of confusion, disorder, and discordant sounds instead of being a place of healing and quiet.

This hospital came to be known simply as Bethlehem with the passing of the years. The longer, fuller name passed from popular usage. Pronounced with only two syllables, as the British speak, the hospital was identified as "Beth-lem." Finally, over long years, the hospital that began as St. Mary of Bethlehem became known as "Bedlam." So came our current word, bedlam.

There is a great deal of bedlam in our world and in our lives. Every Advent season is marked by bedlam. We feel frantic, fractured, and fragmented even as we prepare to celebrate the coming of the Prince of Peace.

While the centuries-old hospital went from Bethlehem to Bedlam, we need to move from bedlam to Bethlehem; our community and our world need to move from bedlam to Bethlehem. The name "Bethlehem" literally means "house of bread." Our lives and our world need the nourishment of Bethlehem, the little town that gave to us the one called "the Bread of Life."

Moving from our bedlam to Bethlehem means to hear the divine announcement that because of a humble and simple appearing, a new possibility of life and peace has been offered in the world. It means that we can join the heavenly chorus and sing: "Glory to God in the highest, and on earth peace."

To journey spiritually to Bethlehem means that at the center of everything is the God of peace. How would you like some of that for Christmas? In the midst of our bedlam, how would you like some of the peace of Bethlehem? It means that the God of peace has the final word. Beyond all of our bedlam, destructive conflicts, and deep disharmony, God comes as the good and heavenly parent to assure us that everything will be okay. God's peace will ultimately triumph.[10]

God's peace triumphs by working its way into our lives. Then, God's peace, the peace that is more than and greater than our understanding, works its way through our lives to others. The way this happens is expressed by the apostle Paul, who urges us to do everything in our power to live in peace with everyone. Are you doing that? How can we? Robert Fulghum expressed part of the answer in his acclaimed book, *All I Really Need to Know I Learned in Kindergarten*:

> Most of what I really need to know about how to live, and what to do, and how to be, I learned in Kindergarten. Wisdom was not at the top of the graduate school mountain, but there in the sandbox at nursery school.
>
> These are the things I learned: Share everything. Play fair. Don't hit people. Put things back where you found them. Clean up your own mess. Don't take things that aren't yours. Say you're sorry when you hurt somebody. Wash your hands before you eat. Flush. Warm cookies and cold milk are good for you. Live a balanced life. Learn some and think some and draw and paint and sing and dance and play and work some every day.
>
> Take a nap every afternoon. When you go out into the world, watch for traffic, hold hands, and stick together.
>
> . . . And it is still true, no matter how old you are, when you go out into the world, it is best to hold hands and stick together.[11]

When President Carter visited Israel and Egypt in March 1978, to mediate between those two countries, he quoted from the philosopher Spinoza, "Peace is not an absence of war; it is a virtue, a state of mind, a disposition for benevolence, confidence, justice." Much more than a cessation of war is meant when the Bible talks about peace. Restrained or controlled hostility is not peace. Paul urges: "Do everything possible on your part to live in peace with everybody" (Rom. 12:18 TEV), he is saying something quite different from the popular philosophy, "don't rock the boat," or "the best way to get along is to go along."

The meaning of peace has Hebrew origin. The Hebrew word is shalom. Shalom expresses the desire and intent of completeness, wholeness, and well being for the individual and for the community. Shalom is the desire that the very best goodness and wholeness happen for a person. Shalom expresses an integration of life that is in harmony, a feeling that one's life is smoothly coordinated, gracefully moving, congruent, and unflappable. That sounds like nirvana, doesn't it? In a sense, to be guided by peace is nirvana. But how can it be? How can our lives be guided by peace?

God wants our lives to be guided by peace. God comes to us, reaches for us. We are wanted by God to be friends with God. This is an awesome thought. God wants us as friends! If you were going to pick your friends, would God be one you choose? Do we pick our friends or do they pick us? Actually, it is both, because one reaches out to another and the other must respond in order for a relationship to have a chance to develop. As we allow God's presence to reach into the depths of our lives, we experience a calmness and serenity that enables us to weather turbulent times in life.

To be guided by peace calls for us to be at peace with ourselves. We must become secure with who we are. We must receive the gift of God's presence and discover that God is seeking to make us whole. "First, keep the peace within yourself, then you can also bring peace to others," observed ecclesiastic Thomas à Kempis. Peace is the cessation of "against-ness." When you're not against yourself or others, you are at peace.[12]

As we realize that God accepts us and wants us as friends, we begin to experience a completeness and wholeness about our lives that causes us to feel settled, calm, and at one with God and God's world. As this happens to us, life around us can be turbulent, stormy, troublesome, but we feel a sense of calmness and serenity that is guiding us through the turmoil and commotion. You have seen that quiet calmness and confidence in the face of a parent or teacher when a crisis arose in life during your childhood. You have seen it in the face of a friend during a time of grave difficulty in your life as that friend stood with you and walked beside you in the midst of agony and anxiety.

Several years ago, a submarine was being tested and had to remain submerged for many hours. When it returned to the harbor, the captain was asked, "How did the terrible storm last night affect you?" The officer looked at him in surprise and exclaimed, "Storm? We didn't even know there was one!" The sub had been so far beneath the surface that it had reached the area known to sailors as "the cushion of the sea." Although the ocean may be whipped into huge waves by high winds, the waters below are never stirred. There is a calmness that cannot be reached by external disturbances when our lives are guided by the peace of God. This is the peace that passes understanding and goes beyond explaining and comprehending.

God wants our lives to be guided by peace. We also must want to be guided by peace in order for it to happen.

There often are images in the Gospels that are connected with a new dwelling place. A peacemaker is one who has found a new home where peace resides and from whence peace is brought into the world.[13]

A young girl was working so diligently at her homework that her father became curious and asked her what she was doing.

"I'm writing a report on the condition of the world and how to bring peace," she replied.

"Isn't that a pretty big order for a young girl?" her father asked.

"Oh, no," she answered, "and don't worry. There are three of us in the class working on it!"

What if three of us were to become as diligent about living in peace with everybody as this young girl was about the assignment she and her two friends were doing together? What a bright, beautiful, safe world this will be as we permit the light of peace to shine in it.

To be guided by peace is to search for and find ways to resolve differences so that relationships win, rather than individuals winning and losing. To be guided by peace is to be able to discover what issues and situations are worth expending large amounts of energy to resolve, and what situations can be allowed to go by the wayside, not worth fanning the flames of fear and emotionalism.

Fearmongering is often the strategy of a political campaign. The result is that people are divided and divisive. The light of peace does not shine on relationships and the emphasis is on individuals winning or losing races rather than finding ways for the nation to win.

In his classic work on the Beatitudes titled *The Heavenly Octave*, F. W. Boreham included this passage:

> The ideal peacemaker is the man who prevents the peace from being broken. To prevent a battle is the best way of winning a battle. I once said to a Jewish rabbi, "I have heard that at a Jewish wedding a glass is broken as part of the symbolism of the ceremony. Is that a fact?" "Of course it is," he replied. "We hold aloft a glass, let it fall and be shattered to atoms, and then, pointing to its fragments, we exhort the young people to guard jealously the sacred relationship into which they have entered since, once it is fractured, it can never be restored."[14]

To be guided by peace is to seek never to break relationships that are established, and it is to be ever seeking to establish new and lasting relationships.

Peace of mind and heart is still one of people's most precious and needed commodities. An extensive survey was conducted in the United States by a leading polling agency. Questionnaires were distributed to people of various ages and occupations. The key question was this: What are you looking for most in life? When the results were compiled, the analysts were surprised. Most of them had expected answers that would suggest materialistic goals, but the top three things that people wanted in life were love, joy, and peace!

What about you? Does this poll register what you are looking for in life? Would you like for your life to be guided by peace? Can it be? Yes, yes it can. When God comes to us, when we invite God to join our lives, to dwell in us, to become a part of us, we are guided by peace and can experience the calmness and serenity we desire. Often, when God comes to us, we aren't interested in God staying with us very long. Perhaps a better way of saying it is we do not stay long with God.

Often, we don't stay long with God because we are afraid. We are afraid of what we might discover. We are not at peace with ourselves. We cannot live in peace with anybody if we are not at peace with ourselves. The journey of peace begins with us. Usually those who are not at peace with themselves are afraid. Fear governs their lives. Henri Nouwen observed:

> Those who are in favor of fighting are dwelling in a house that is ruled by fear. It is not difficult to see that. Panic, fear, and anxiety are not part of peacemaking. Fear is a tempting, perhaps the most tempting, force to use for peacemaking. When fear is the method used for making peace, anything but peace will result. Those who take this approach remain captives to the strategies of those who want to fight.[15]

Many years ago, Gustave Valbert reported in the *Moscow Gazette* that "From the year 1496 B.C. to A.D. 1861, in 3358 years there were 227 years of peace and 3,130 years of war, or 13 years of war to every year of peace. Within the last three centuries, there have been 286 wars in Europe." Valbert also noted that from the year 1500 B.C. to A.D. 1860 more than 8000 treaties of peace, meant to remain in force forever, were concluded. The average time they remained in force was two years.[16]

Renowned pastor Halford Luccock said that he was shopping during the Christmas rush and bumped into a woman and spilled her packages in every direction. He helped her gather them up and apologized. She said, "Oh, how I hate Christmas. It turns everything around in life." That is what the Advent season is all about. God comes into the world and seeks to come into our lives. Everything in life is turned around when God comes to our lives. God calls for us to relate in a different way to people and to nations. God comes to the world and God's name is Prince of Peace. God turns everything around in our lives with regard to the ways we relate. God calls for righteousness and justice to kiss in our lives. Righteousness and justice can kiss in our lives only when we are seeking to wage peace. Peace must be waged in our minds, because only then will we put a stop to our rhetoric of retaliation that continues to escalate division and destruction.

God has done a very dangerous thing. God has provided the instruction and the direction for waging peace, but God has left it up to us to be the makers of peace. Those who make peace are the ones who are called the children of God. What Jimmy Breslin, an Irish writer, said about his fellow citizens, too often is descriptive of us. Breslin wrote, "Northern Ireland has some of the best Catholics and best Protestants in the world—and not a Christian among them."

Advent represents the coming of God to our lives. If we invite God to dwell with us, we will discover that God's dwelling with us turns everything around in our lives, not the least of which will be the call for us to get the story right and permit the light of peace to guide us from bedlam to Bethlehem.

To journey spiritually to Bethlehem means that at the center of everything is the God of peace. In the midst of our bedlam, how would you like some of the peace of Bethlehem? It means that the God of peace has the final word. Beyond all of our bedlam, destructive conflicts, and deep disharmony, God comes as the good and heavenly parent to give us the light of peace that casts out the darkness of fear and animosity and hostility.

God dwells with us and God's presence turns everything around. For us to call God "Prince of Peace" is for us to acknowledge one who has authority for completeness and wholeness. The authority of the Prince of Peace becomes authentic in our lives as we seek peace and, inasmuch as is possible for us, we live in peace with everybody. Then, even in the midst of a terrible, devastating storm, we will experience completeness and wholeness, peace that passes understanding. Indeed, then the light of peace will shine in our lives and through our lives to others because no one takes a light and hides it. Rather, the light of peace is set aglow in our lives and brings light to our lives and Bethlehem to our bedlam.

JUSTICE

The world needs peace, peace with justice. The biblical idea of justice is fidelity to the demands of a relationship. The Israelites were to be parents to those without parents and to feed the stranger, not because the orphan or outsider deserved it, but because this was the way God acted toward Israel. The Jews were to image the justice of God. The just disciple of Jesus has made a covenant with God; this covenant demands that we treat other women and men as God wants them treated in God's covenant plan.

To be in right relationship with God is to love God with our whole heart, mind, and soul and to love our fellow human beings as ourselves. Loving your sisters and brothers is like loving God. Walter Burghardt writes, "In our efforts for justice, we Christians are not simply social workers, imperative as social work is, whatever one's belief or unbelief. We are involved because we want to live the second great commandment. As for the Jewish people, so for us: Not to execute justice is not to worship God."[17]

The intent of biblical religion has never been the avoidance of conflict at any cost. Jesus once said, "Woe to you when all men speak well of you, for so their fathers did to the false prophets" (Lk. 6:26 RSV). One well-known theologian and preacher, after hearing a sermon marked by eloquence and soothing charm, wrote, "Lord preserve me from eloquence . . . let my words have a jagged edge."[18]

George Carey expresses clearly that doing justice is being faithful followers of Christ. He writes, "Jesus proclaimed a justice which undercuts self-righteousness, self-satisfaction, and self-justification. Jesus never suggests to his followers that by doing what he says they will receive rewards in this life. Loving enemies is not guaranteed to turn their hearts. They might only increase their persecution. Turning the other cheek is not recommended for its prudence. It is a proclamation of a coming kingdom, which throws us back always to examine our own motives in the light of the pure goodness of God."[19]

Minister and writer Letty Russell tells about three churches in her home state of Connecticut and their efforts to call a pastor. One church called a pastor and then rescinded the call before she could accept. They had read about her work with another pastor on peace and justice issues and didn't want any "troublemaker" around. Another formed a special committee to discuss whether the pastor they were calling would be able to separate concern for peace from concern for religion. Yet another placed an invitation in the local newspaper of a struggling, old industrial town in the Northeast to come and worship where the town's "first families have worshiped for centuries."

Only true repentance and willingness to be in, but not of, the world will lead people to search for just and responsible relationships in community. Robert Bellah calls this the difference between community and lifestyle. In *Habits of the Heart*, Bellah says that community attempts to be an inclusive whole, while lifestyle is "fundamentally segmental and celebrates the narcissism of similarity."[20]

Imaginative and constructive repentance leads us toward a desire for social transformation, beginning with the church. But this is very difficult and requires a willingness to risk the suffering that comes to those who seek to do justice by challenging and changing the status quo of any society. Adrienne Rich has pointed out in *Blood, Bread, and Poetry* that she was greatly helped in making a decision to risk her own life by a quotation from writer

James Baldwin: "Any real change implies the break up of the world as one has always known it, the loss of all that gave one an identity, the end of safety."[21]

The world as we know it is unjust, and to share with God in the building of a community of justice is to call for a break up of the world as we know it and for a new creation.[22] The prophet Amos states clearly the evidence of injustice found in any generation:

> They hate him who reproves in the gate, and they abhor him who speaks the truth. Therefore because you trample upon the poor and take from him exactions of wheat, you have built houses of hewn stone, but you shall not dwell in them; you have planted pleasant vineyards, but you shall not drink their wine. For I know how many are your transgressions, and how great are your sins—you who afflict the righteous, who take a bribe, and turn aside the needy in the gate. Therefore he who is prudent will keep silent in such a time; for it an evil time. (Amos 5:10–13 RSV)

A repeated theme that Amos uses for his people to have life is for them to "seek the Lord." They are urged to go to some sanctuary or priest or prophet and offer a sacrifice or receive an oracle. The problem was that the people in Amos's day were going to places of worship to go through the motions of worship. They were confused and wrong when they thought what God wanted was perfunctory observance of religious rituals.

Their lives had become flooded by injustice. Amos spoke a stern word of correction to them, pointing out that life must be marked by justice, righteousness, and goodness or it did not matter when, where, or how many religious services they attended.

True seeking of God is an inward journey that results in outward change. If we harbor prejudice, are racist and classist in our attitudes and actions, we have not been saved, have not been made whole and complete by the love and grace of God. The judgment of God is upon us. God's judgment is the logical consequences and results of our attitudes and actions.

If we continue to oppress people, treat them with disrespect, and regard them as second- or third-class citizens, the pressure within them will become so intense that they will erupt in anger and rage. Destruction will reign. The mandate of love is that if God loves people and cares for them we are to do the same. To refuse to do so is to say we have not been saved.

Amos said that his people had turned justice into wormwood. Wormwood was a plant that had a bitter and sometimes harmful juice. Justice is sweet and satisfying; injustice is bitter and frustrating. Amos also pointed out that his people had thrown down righteousness. They had caused righteousness to rest, to lie prone on the ground rather than standing erect as righteousness is supposed to do. Righteousness means to maintain the proper relationship with other people and with God.

The wealthy were oppressing the poor, taking and giving bribes, and keeping the poor from getting justice in the courts. Amos indicated directly that the rich believed and operated by another golden rule: Those with the gold, rule. Have we not sensed and seen the same thing in our culture? Are we not aware of situations where only those with a lot of money could afford to have a matter decided in court? Have there been injustices that people made no attempt to correct because they did not have the money necessary for good legal counsel? When Amos saw the local courts corrupted, he knew that sin was not confined to the cultic and political leaders but that it had permeated the whole fabric of society.

Amos also suggested that people who knew injustices were taking place kept their mouths shut during such evil times because that was the "smart" thing to do. In light of all that Amos was saying, this must have been a sarcastic statement made with tongue in cheek. Amos was bemoaning the fact that his nation had come to a time when it was dangerous to speak the truth (5:13). Prophets and honest free men who spoke the truth were jeopardizing their lives. A society commits a mortal sin when the word of truth is stifled.

Amos urges his hearers to seek life three times in this chapter. Seeking life is directly tied to relating to God and developing authentic religion. Genuine religion is expressed when a person is in proper personal relationship with God and with fellow human beings. There are vertical and horizontal dimensions of authentic religion.

Amos began the fifth chapter of his writing singing a funeral song over his fallen nation. It had fallen because of injustice that those in power and control were inflicting on fellow citizens. Amos had a different view than most about whom God's enemies were. He pointed out that judgment and accountability were inevitable. He said that a person might run away from a lion only to be overtaken at another point by a bear. Or a person might flee to his home for safety only to be bitten by a snake at the least suspecting moment. Many people are eager for the day of Yahweh, the Day of Judgment and accountability. Usually those who are most eager for that day think they are protected and exempt from any accountability or consequences. Amos said that day would be a day of reckoning for everybody, certainly and especially for those who have been unjust and unrighteous.

Amos stripped away the doctrine of election or "chosen-ness" related to birth or status. He established justice and righteousness as indispensable. He said God hated, despised, and rejected the worship services of the people because the people were hypocritical and incongruent. He said the songs of the people were noisy, not because the singers and instruments were musically off-key, but because they were socially and spiritually out of tune.

Amos said that righteousness should be a perennial stream and that justice should flow naturally and unimpeded through the courts and the marketplace. Amos's words, spoken 2,800 years ago, are as relevant as today's headlines.

What the world needs now is for you and me to see that justice flows freely in our lives and that we relate in the right way to everybody. We also need to challenge and confront people when they stop justice and when they do not relate in the right way to others.

Here are some things we can do. We must become aware of the prejudices we feel. The stronger or more often we need to say that we aren't prejudiced, the more likely we protest too much and are more prejudiced than we have been willing to see or admit. You know the old adage that suggests that a person "protests too much." Be willing to see differences between yourself and people of another color and between yourself and people in a different economic class. But don't stereotype people on the basis of color or class. Do not conclude that all black people think or act or speak a certain way. Do not conclude that all people of low income are ignorant or stupid.

A second thing to do is when you hear a prejudiced or racist statement being made, counter that statement or act by speaking out in opposition. To be silent is to give consent. People will interpret your silence as agreeing with them.

The caption beside a picture in the May 11, 1992, issue of *Newsweek*, in the height of riots in Los Angeles, read, "The water from one bucket, thrown by one man, couldn't douse the flames that shot from the neighborhood store. Streets swarming with defiant youths, whole city blocks on fire, looters streaming out of stores with anything they could carry—these were images the nation hadn't seen for years and had hoped never to see again. The shock of the verdict in the Rodney King beating case was overtaken only by the shock at the lawlessness that broke out in Los Angeles."[23]

One person's voice cannot quell the racism in this country or any country. But the place to start is with my voice. I can quell the noise and voice of racism that comes from me by becoming more aware of my prejudice. Then I can add my voice of justice and righteousness to your voice and the voices of others by countering injustice, unrighteousness, prejudice, and racism whenever and wherever it is spoken. What the world needs now is justice. The world needs your voice and my voice speaking out for justice. Only as justice flows from us can it form a never-ending stream that rolls down like water pouring over the lives of people everywhere.

LOVE

Late in the 1960s, Dionne Warwick sang, "What the World Needs Now Is Love." Nearly forty years later, the need is as strong and as relevant as ever. What greater need is there anywhere for anything in the world than the need for love? Children need love. Spouses need love. Leaders and followers, teachers and students, men and women, the upwardly mobile and down-wardly disheartened need love.

Think about it. Have you ever been loved unconditionally? Has someone ever cared deeply about your well-being, put himself out for you without considering at all what it was costing him, and nothing was expected, demanded, or required of you in return? Who has ever treated you this way? Who have you treated this way? If strings and conditions are attached to what someone says is love, it isn't love. Call it control. Call it manipulation. Call it coercion, but don't call it love.

Living intentionally to love another unconditionally is not without risk, including the strong possibilities of rejection and persecution. But the benefits to the one loved are immeasurable. Read this well-known, anonymously written poem about love:

> I love you, not only for what you are,
> But for what I am when I am with you,
> I love you not only for what you have
> Made of your self, but for what you are
> Making of me, I love you because you are
> Helping me make of the lumber of my life,
> Not a tavern but a temple.

When Queen Victoria of England pinned one of England's highest awards on Helen Keller, she asked her, "How do you account for your remarkable accomplishments in life? How do you explain the fact that even though you were both blind and deaf, you were able to accomplish so much?" Without a moment's hesitation, Helen Keller said, "If it had not been for Anne Sullivan, the name of Helen Keller would have remained unknown." While we know Helen Keller's story, most of us do not know who saw the potential in Keller's teacher, Anne Sullivan. As a young girl, Anne Sullivan was known as "Little Annie." She was diagnosed as being hopelessly insane and was locked in the basement of a mental institution outside of Boston. Little Annie would, on occasion, violently attack anyone who came near her. At other times she would completely ignore them.

An elderly nurse believed there was hope for the child and felt she could communicate love and hope to her. The nurse visited Little Annie daily, but for a long time Little Annie gave no indication she was aware of her presence. The elderly nurse persisted and repeatedly brought some cookies and left them in her room. Soon the doctors in the institution noticed a change. After a period of time, they moved Little Annie upstairs. Finally the day came when this seemingly "hopeless case" was released. Filled with compassion for others because of her institutional experience, Little Annie, Anne Sullivan, wanted to help others. Therefore, it was Anne Sullivan who saw the great potential in Helen Keller. She loved her, disciplined her, played, prayed, pushed, and worked with her until the flickering candle that was her life became a beacon that helped light the pathway and lighten the burdens of people all over the world. But first, there was the elderly nurse, then Anne

Sullivan, then Helen Keller, and finally each one of us, and additional millions, who have been influenced by the example of Helen Keller.[24]

Jesus' lifestyle signaled the liberation that occurs with love. He demonstrated by word and deed the stages through which the law of retaliation had passed and how it finally came to rest in the universal love of God. The stages are unlimited retaliation, limited retaliation, limited love, and unlimited love.

No limit is placed on revenge in unlimited retaliation. If someone puts out your eye then, if at all possible, you put out both of theirs. All is fair in unlimited retaliation. Might makes right in the sense that if one is able to inflict more injury than he receives, then he has the right to do it. The rule is: Do unto others so they cannot do unto you. Brief reflection causes many to conclude there is a better way.

Limited retaliation is a better way. Limited retaliation says that if someone knocks one of your teeth out, you can retaliate by knocking out one of his. You cannot knock out all of his teeth. In other words, get even, but no more. The rule is: Do unto others as they do unto you. Limited retaliation is better than unlimited retaliation, but if this rule is followed, as Gandhi noted, the world becomes filled with blind, toothless people.

The culture out of which the Hebrew Scriptures were formed developed a better way, the way of limited love. Limited love is stated as "You have heard it that it was said, 'You shall love your neighbor and hate your enemy'" (Mt. 5:43 RSV). If a neighbor caused injury, he might be forgiven, but if an enemy caused injury, then give him the works. An enemy could be punished as harshly and as drastically as desired. In those days, a neighbor was a Jew and an enemy was a Gentile. For too many of us today, a neighbor is a white, Anglo-Saxon Protestant and an enemy is anyone else. The rule of limited love is: Do unto your enemies as they do to you. The result is a double standard, one for people who are known and liked and another for those unknown or disliked.

Jesus' intention was to free people from the bondage of retaliation and limited love. His method was never to pay back evil with evil, but to return good for evil, to turn the other cheek, and to go the second mile. His lifestyle and his instructions to disciples added up to a person permitting others to impose on him. This approach expresses unlimited love and involves loving outsiders and praying for those who try to do others in. We tend to go along with this unlimited love approach as long as the enemy is weaker than we are because turning the cheek won't hurt too much. We claim this approach will not work with a bigger, stronger enemy.

An Austrian colonel told of his orders to march against the little town of Tyrol and lay siege to it. One prisoner who had been captured said, "You'll never take that town because they have an invincible leader." No one seemed to know what the prisoner meant or who the leader was. The colonel doubled his preparation. As they descended through the pass in the Alps, the cattle were still in the field and the women and children, and even the men, were at work in the fields. An ambush was apparent. As the soldiers drew near the town, they passed people on the road who smiled and greeted them and went on their way.

Finally, the soldiers reached the town and clattered up the street. People came to their windows and doorways. Some looked a little startled and then went on their way. The soldiers arrived at the town hall. Out came an old white-haired man followed by ten men in peasant clothes. The old man walked to the colonel and extended his hand. The colonel asked, "Where are your soldiers?"

The old man replied, "Why, don't you know that we have none?"

"But we have come to take this town," exclaimed the colonel.

"Well, no one will stop you."

"Are there none here to fight?" asked the colonel.

The old man responded, "No, there is no one here to fight. We have chosen Christ for our leader and he taught people another way." The colonel and his soldiers left the town unmolested. It was impossible to take it.

Our claim is that the way of unlimited love is impractical. All that happens in such an approach is that people get nailed. That is true. The road to freedom that Jesus invites us to walk is not a road to practicality by the world's standards. Jesus tells us to love our enemies because that attitude is essential if we are to create peace. Peace takes root in the soil of righteousness and is watered by mercy and forgiveness. It is easier to promote strife than to create peace. It does take two to make a quarrel, but even my most hostile antagonist cannot break the peace unless I collaborate with him. If I resolve to make peace, peace will be made.

This unconditional love that Jesus talked about, taught, and lived was wrapped and tied with forgiveness. Only genuine, authentic, unconditional love has the instinct, the insight, and the courage to forgive.

Forgiveness is a rare commodity in our society. People bury the hatchet, but carefully tuck away the map where the hidden hatchet lies. Forgiveness is essential for relationships to be maintained because hurt and estrangement occur that can only be dealt with by forgiveness. Forgiveness is a change of attitude within the one wronged. It means to forego all private revenge and to remit the right to retaliate. When one has been wronged, she has every justification to get even. The law is on her side. Friends support her. Often, even her enemies will admit she has a point. Forgiveness involves acknowledgement that one has been hurt and estranged and to become aware that the one who caused the estrangement has been hurt by causing the estrangement. Forgiveness is an unashamed admission that the relationship is more important than revenge or retaliation.

There are some misconceptions about forgiveness. "Forgive and forget" is sometimes unsolicited advice offered by bystanders, but this is impossible unless a person experiences selective amnesia. How will the offended person become aware of any contribution he made to the estrangement if he forgets the entire situation? To forgive neither cancels nor undoes the damage or the offense; rather, the offended person forgoes the attempt to get even and seeks to continue the relationship. Forgiveness and forgetfulness are not synonymous. A second misconception is that forgiveness means to pass over a broken relationship and say, "It really doesn't matter." Relationships do matter and it is the admission of their importance that will cause one to seek to forgive another, rather than to gloss over the breach. A third misconception of forgiveness is expressed as condescension and goes like this: "You have hurt me deeply, but I will bear it." This is merely a form of one-upmanship that continually reminds the offender of his offense. It keeps the estranged feelings buried alive by establishing a superior-to-inferior relationship. The offended one uses his position of having been offended to wield power over the one who caused the estrangement. Forgiveness is not authentic when the offended person maintains a superior position by claiming to forgive, saying the offense doesn't matter, or saying he will bear the hurt.

We are captives of condemnation, blaming others as well as ourselves. There is a way out of this hell and it is wrapped in the nature of mercy and forgiveness. It is the nature of mercy and forgiveness that receiving mercy is related directly to giving forgiveness. Those who demonstrate mercy also receive mercy. One does not earn forgiveness; that would be mercy by reward. The condition of the unmerciful person is such that he is incapable of receiving mercy. One who is incapable of giving forgiveness is incapable of receiving mercy because he is blind both to what mercy is and to his need for it. What blocks the flow of mercy from a person also blocks its flow back to him. The law of physics is that for every action there is a reaction. If there is no action, then there is no reaction. Without the action of giving mercy, there is no reaction of receiving mercy.

The willingness to forgive is limitless. Love begins as an attitude and ends in an action. Peter asked Jesus if seven times was the limit of forgiveness (Mt. 18:21). Jesus responded that one ought to forgive either seventy times seven or seventy-seven times, the exact translation is unclear. Whether to forgive 77 times or 490 times is not the point because to keep count reveals one's interest in retaliation rather than forgiveness. Instead of endless revenge, the disciple of Christ is to practice endless forgiveness.

The way of the world calls for retaliation, an eye for an eye and a tooth for a tooth. Retaliation produces revenge and we become captives of condemnation. Jesus spoke a word that cut across the way of the world. He said the way out of hell is paved with love that produces forgiveness. Truly to forgive another is to lay down one's life for the benefit of the relationship with that person. Jesus spoke a lasting word about love that liberates people from condemnation.

Poet Rainer Maria Rilke said in a letter to a young friend, "For one human being to love another . . . is perhaps the most difficult of all our tasks, the ultimate, the last test and proof, the work for which all other work is but preparation." That is a proper assessment—we work all our lives preparing to love.[25] Therein lies our salvation. Only through love are we given enough space to get away from doing evil. Holocaust survivor Viktor Frankl said, "The salvation of man is through love and in love."[26]

An ingenious teenager, tired of reading bedtime stories to his little sister, decided to record several of her favorite stories on tape. He told her, "Now you can hear your stories anytime you want. Isn't that great?" She looked at the machine for a moment and then replied, "No. It hasn't got a lap." We all need a lap. We all need the closeness of relationship. We all need to know we are loved.

John of the Cross, Spanish mystic and poet, said that in the end, we would be judged on one thing only: our love. Fifteen years after Julian of Norwich's contemplative of the fourteenth century revelations, God explained them to her in these words: "Love was their meaning. Love showed them to you. They were shown to you for Love." Francis de Sales ended his greatest treatise with a hymn: "Ah, come Holy Spirit, and inflame our hearts with your love. To love or to die!"

With each returning glance toward the ever-present love of God, we see through the eyes of the prodigal child that God is touched, overjoyed, helplessly, hopelessly in love with us. There is nothing that can change this continual openness of God to us: nothing that we can do, nothing that can be done to us. And there is nothing that can ever separate us from it. As Paul continued in his speech to the Athenians, "Yet he is not far from each one of us, for 'In him we live and move and have our very being'" (Acts 17:27–28 RSV). We can deny or forget the irrevocable reality of God's immediate love, and we will certainly deny our own lovability and the spirit within us that keeps yearning God-ward, but such denial is only a matter of consciousness. It does not change the truth. The truth is that we are created out of love, for the purpose of love, and that we live every instant of our lives within love. [27]

What the world needs now is faith, peace, justice, and love, but the greatest of these is love. The world needs unconditional, self-giving, life-giving love, the bounteous, generous, unconditional love of God. What the world needs now is for people to experience this unconditional love in the flesh and blood of relationships with fellow human beings. That is how the message of God's love to the world can be read, received, understood, and believed. May the love of God flow to you and to me and through you and me out into the parched world, nourishing and nurturing the world with just what it needs. Let us go to the world with love.

QUESTIONS TO PONDER

1. What do you think the world needs?

2. How can you be a partner with God in providing what the world needs?

3. What does it mean to you to forgive and forget?

4. Why is it so difficult to forgive and forget?

5. How have you experienced the stages of the law of retaliation?

6. Why is it so difficult to live and communicate unlimited love?

7. Who has loved you unconditionally?

8. How can that person be a model for you to love others unconditionally?

NOTES

Preface

   1. Marcus J. Borg, *The God We Never Knew: Beyond Dogmatic Religion to a More Authentic Contemporary Faith* (San Francisco: HarperSanFrancisco, 1997), 32.

Chapter 1

   1. Grady Nutt, *Agaperos* (Nashville, Tenn.: Broadman, 1977), 86.

   2. Arthur Gordon, *A Touch of Wonder: A Book to Help People Stay in Love with Life* (Old Tappan, N. J.: H. Revell, 1974), 11.

Chapter 2

   1. Nutt, *Agaperos*, 59.

   2. Gordon, *A Touch of Wonder*, 179.

Chapter 3

   1. There is an excellent Christmas drama by this name that has appeared on television and been performed in theaters and churches throughout the world.

   2. Robert McAfee Brown, *Unexpected News: Reading the Bible with Third World Eyes* (Philadelphia: Westminster Press, 1984), 77.

   3. Kahlil Gibran, *The Prophet* (New York: Knopf, 1971), 18–19.

4. W. Hugh Missildine, *Your Inner Child of the Past* (New York: Simon & Schuster, 1963), 199.

5. Thomas Merton made this comment to seminarians visiting the monastery in Bardstown, Kentucky, in the spring of 1970.

6. This observation about Joseph was made in an Advent sermon in 1971 by Dr. Hull while he was professor of New Testament interpretation at Southern Baptist Theological Seminary in Louisville, Kentucky. I was a student there at the time.

7. Kenneth E. Bailey, "The Manger and the Inn: A Middle Eastern View of the Birth Story of Jesus," *The Presbyterian Outlook* 170, no. 1 (Jan. 4–11, 1988): 8–9.

8. Ibid., 8.

9. Ibid., 9.

10. The ideas expressed in the previous paragraphs about being home for Christmas come from a sermon by John Killinger, "Home for Christmas," *Pulpit Digest* 76, no. 542 (Nov./Dec. 1996), 12–14.

11. I remember reading this idea of Inge's in an early edition of *The Living Pulpit.*

Chapter 4
1. Edwin Markham, "How the Great Guest Came," *The Shoes of Happiness and Other Poems: The Third Book of Verse by Edwin Markham* (Garden City, N.Y.: Doubleday, Page & Co., 1915), 59–60.

Chapter 5
1. James Dittes, *Minister on the Spot* (Philadelphia: The Pilgrim Press, 1970), 54.

2. I saw this statement on a wall in a museum in Novosibirsk, Siberia, in May of 1983.

3. John Killinger, *Fundamentals of Preaching* (Minneapolis: Fortress Press, 1996), 87.

4. From John Blackwell, pastor of Mission Bell United Methodist Church, Phoenix, Arizona, in an article written for *Pulpit Digest* circa 1991. I am unable to locate the issue where I first read this.

Chapter 6

1. Edwin Markham, "Outwitted," *The Shoes of Happiness and Other Poems*, 1.

2. I read this story by Mark Trotter in an issue of *Pulpit Digest* circa 1990.

3. James W. Fowler, *Stages of Faith: The Psychology of Human Development and the Quest for Meaning* (San Francisco: Harper & Row, 1981), 5.

4. Ibid., 4.

5. Wilfred Cantwell Smith, *The Meaning and End of Religion: A New Approach to the Religious Traditions of Mankind* (New York: Macmillan, 1963), 12.

6. Clarence Jordan, qtd. in Walter Knight, "Waging Peace," *Peacework*, 12 (May 1985): 3. This is a newsletter published by Baptist Peace Fellowship of North America.

7. Thomas C. Oden, *First and Second Timothy and Titus*, Interpretation: A Bible Commentary for Teaching and Preaching, ed. James Luther Mays (Louisville, Ky.: John Knox, 1989), 172.

8. Alice Walker, *The Color Purple: A Novel* (New York: Harcourt Brace Jovanovich, 1987), 165.

9. G. K. Chesterton, *What's Wrong with the World?* (New York: Dodd, Mead, and Co., 1910), 48.

10. Fred Andrea, "From the Pastor's Study," *The Calendar* 56, no. 50 (18 Dec. 1991): 2.

11. Robert Fulghum, *All I Really Need to Know I Learned in Kindergarten: Uncommon Thoughts on Common Things* (New York: Villard Books, 1989), 6–8.

12. John-Roger and Peter McWilliams, *Life 101: Everything We Wish We Had Learned about Life in School—But Didn't* (Los Angeles: Prelude, 1990), 373.

13. Henry Nouwen, "A Spirituality of Peacemaking," *Harvard Divinity Bulletin* 16, no. 1 (Oct./Nov. 1985): 6.

14. F. W. Boreham, *The Heavenly Octave: A Study of the Beatitudes* (New York: Abingdon Press, 1936), 95.

15. Nouwen, "A Spirituality of Peacemaking," 6.

16. This information about Gustave Valbert came from a computer software program called *Biblical Illustrator for Windows*, dist. Parsons Software (Hiawatha, Ia., 1999).

17. Walter J. Burghardt, S.J., "Justice in God's Own Book," *The Living Pulpit* 2, no. 1 (Jan.–Mar. 1993): 5.

18. James Limburg, "Amos," *Hosea-Micah*, Interpretation: A Bible Commentary for Teaching and Preaching, ed. James Luther Mays (Atlanta: John Knox, 1988), 119.

19. George Carey, "God, Goodness, and Justice," *The Living Pulpit* 2, no. 1 (Jan.–Mar. 1993): 7.

20. Robert Bellah, *Habits of the Heart: Individualism and Commitment in American Life* (Berkeley: University of California Press, 1985), 139.

21. Adrienne Rich, *Blood, Bread, and Poetry: Selected Prose, 1979–1985* (New York: Norton, 1986), 79.

22. Letty M. Russell, "Justice and the Double Sin of the Church," *The Living Pulpit* 2, no. 1 (Jan.–Mar.1993): 18–19.

23. J. Alter, "TV and the 'Firebell,'" *Newsweek*, May 11, 1992, 43.

24. Jeffrey Holland, "Whose Children Are These? A Family Connection," *Vital Speeches of the Day* 54(7 July 1988): 558.

25. John Killinger, *For God's Sake, Be Human* (Waco, Tex.: Word Books, 1970), 78.

26. Qtd. by Killinger, ibid., 82.

27. Gerald May, "To Love—Or to Die," *Shalem News* 13, no.1 (Feb. 1989): 5.

BIBLIOGRAPHY

Alter, J. "TV and the 'Firebell.'" *Newsweek* . May 11, 1992. 43.

Andrea, Fred. "From the Pastor's Study." *The Calendar* 56, no. 50 (18 Dec. 1991): 2.

Bailey, Kenneth E. "The Manger and the Inn: A Middle Eastern View of the Birth Story of Jesus." *The Presbyterian Outlook* 170, no. 1 (Jan. 4–11, 1988): 8–9.

Bellah, Robert N. *Habits of the Heart: Individualism and Commitment in American Life*. Berkeley: University of California Press, 1985.

Boreham, F. W. *The Heavenly Octave: A Study of the Beatitudes* . New York: Abingdon Press, 1936.

Borg, Marcus J. *The God We Never Knew: Beyond Dogmatic Religion to a More Authentic Contemporary Faith*. San Francisco: HarperSanFrancisco, 1997.

Brown, Robert McAfee. *Unexpected News: Reading the Bible with Third World Eyes* . Philadelphia: Westminster Press, 1984.

Burghardt, Walter J., S.J. "Justice in God's Own Book." *The Living Pulpit* 2, no. 1 (Jan.–Mar. 1993): 5.

Carey, George. "God, Goodness, and Justice." *The Living Pulpit* 2, no.1 (Jan.–Mar. 1993).

Chesterton, G. K. *What's Wrong with the World?* New York: Dodd, Mead and Co., 1910.

Dittes, James E. *Minister on the Spot*. Philadelphia: The Pilgrim Press, 1970.

Fowler, James W. *Stages of Faith: The Psychology of Human Development and the Quest for Meaning*. San Francisco: Harper & Row, 1981.

Fulghum, Robert. *All I Really Need to Know I Learned in Kindergarten: Uncommon Thoughts on Common Things*. New York: Villard, 1989.

Gibran, Kahlil. *The Prophet*. New York: Knopf, 1971.

Gordon, Arthur. *A Touch of Wonder: A Book to Help People Stay in Love with Life*. Old Tappan, N. J.: H. Revell, 1974.

Holland, Jeffrey. "Whose Children Are These? A Family Connection." *Vital Speeches of the Day* 54 (7 July 1988).

Killinger, John. *For God's Sake, Be Human*. Waco, Tex.: Word Books, 1970.

———. *Fundamentals of Preaching*. 2nd ed. Minneapolis: Fortress Press, 1996.

———. "Home for Christmas." *Pulpit Digest* 76, no. 542 (Nov./Dec., 1996): 12–14.

Knight, Walter. "Waging Peace." *Peacework* 12 (May 1985): 3–4.

Limburg, James. "Amos." *Hosea-Micah*. Interpretation: A Bible Commentary for Teaching and Preaching. Ed. James Luther Mays. Atlanta: John Knox, 1988. 79–126.

Markham, Edwin. *The Shoes of Happiness and Other Poems: The Third Book of Verse by Edwin Markham*. Garden City, N.Y.: Doubleday, Page & Co., 1915.

May, Gerald. "To Love—Or to Die." *Shalem News* 13, no. 1. (Feb. 1989): 5.

McWilliams, Peter, and John–Roger. *Life 101: Everything We Wish We Had Learned about Life in School—But Didn't*. Los Angeles: Prelude, 1990.

Missildine, W. Hugh. *Your Inner Child of the Past*. New York: Simon & Schuster, 1963.

Nouwen, Henry. "A Spirituality of Peacemaking." *Harvard Divinity Bulletin* 16, no. 1 (Oct./Nov. 1985): 5–6.

Nutt, Grady. *Agaperos*. Nashville: Broadman, 1977.

Oden, Thomas. *First and Second Timothy and Titus.* Interpretation: A Bible Commentary for Teaching and Preaching. Ed. James Luther Mays. Louisville, Ky.: John Knox, 1989.

Rich, Adrienne. *Blood, Bread, and Poetry: Selected Prose, 1979–1985*. New York: Norton, 1986.

Russell, Letty M. "Justice and the Double Sin of the Church." *The Living Pulpit* 2, no. 1. (Jan.–Mar. 1993): 18–19.

Smith, Wilfred Cantwell. *The Meaning and End of Religion: A New Approach to the Religious Traditions of Mankind*. New York: Macmillan, 1963.

Walker, Alice. *The Color Purple: A Novel*. New York: Harcourt Brace Jovanovich, 1987.

OTHER BOOKS BY
THE PILGRIM PRESS

IN SEARCH OF FAITH
Profiles of Biblical Seekers
HOWARD W. ROBERTS
0-8298-1412-4/paper/176 pages/$12.00

In Search of Faith is an exploration of the biblical characters who struggled to define their faith lives. Its purpose is to help readers identify with biblical characters, discover kinship with seekers of another era, and to read about themselves in these stories.

PRAYING LIKE JESUS
HOWARD W. ROBERTS
0-8298-1326-8/paper/160 pages/$15.95

Jesus prayed his most agonizing prayer in the Garden of Gethsemane. His genuine emotion and passion are expressed to God as he faces certain death. *Praying Like Jesus* will lead readers to pray with that same depth—for friends and enemies, for people in need, and for the healing of the world.

To place an order call 800.537.3394 or visit our Web site at

<www.pilgrimpress.org>.